Visual Collaboration

A Powerful Toolkit for Improving Meetings, Projects, and Processes

Ole Qvist-Sørensen and Loa Baastrup
Illustrated by Sofie Lind Mesterton

"This book is structured in a very pedagogical and logical way. It is clear and easy to understand and richly illustrated. You quickly experience success with drawing. It is a unique handbook that provides many years of experience from practice in process design and visual facilitation. I highly recommend Visual Collaboration to meeting leaders, process designers, teachers and anyone interested in learning."

Lotte Darsø, Associate Professor, University of Aarhus, Author of *Artful Creation*

"Visual collaboration *enables amazing new forms of collaboration and innovation in organizations. I've had the privilege of working with the authors many times, and this book gives anyone the ability to bring their unique skills and capabilities into their own work.*"

Ron Volpe, Global Vice President Apps Business Development, Tradeshift

"This book shows how drawings and visualization increase the bandwidth of collaboration. Something we desperately need, when we work in complex situations. The book is a must-read and has become an essential part of our company toolbox."

Henrik Challis, Senior Consultant in Organization Transformation, Co-Founder, Emerging

"When I first came across visual facilitation, it was a bonus if a consultant were able to draw and visualize for clients. Today it is a must. This is a very impressive book; it shows how much is possible and should be on every consultant's bookshelf!"

Jacob Storch, Phd, Entrepreneur, Founder, Joint Action and Attractor

"Visual Collaboration *is a book I will not only read; I will use it. I want to become better at sketching, and I want to learn how to use visualizations more. A picture is worth a thousand words.*"

Lars Kolind, former CEO, Oticon, Board Member, Entrepreneur and Author of *Unboss*

"As a process consultant on participatory processes and strategic conversations, I have learned that visualization promotes collective understanding and memory. Visual Collaboration *gives an overview and an introduction to the use of visual tools and techniques in an educational and simple way. It speaks to different levels of experience and practice, whether you are a beginner or a more experienced user.*"

Monica Nissen, Process Consultant, Co-Founder, InterChange

"I have followed the evolution of the methods described in Visual Collaboration *since its earliest days. I am delighted to see its' core message regarding the power of 'making conversations visible' to support collaborative innovation and constructive change in organizations and communities being communicated in engaging and creative ways that can support both the novice and experienced practitioner. The global spread of the World Cafe approach to strategic dialogue and collective intelligence has benefited enormously from the approaches described in this important contribution to the field.*"

Juanita Brown PhD, Co-Founder, The World Cafe

"Visual Collaboration *is an inspiring guide for anyone who is interested in a more visual approach to organizing and hosting meetings and workshops. The book walks the reader step-by-step from discovering a new visual language to enabling others to work more visually. As a reader one doesn't only find helpful hands-on tips but also inspirational templates which can be easily customized for any kind of meeting and workshop.*"

Donato Carparelli, Head Global Product Innovation, Schindler Elevator Ltd

For general information on our other products and services or for technical support, please contact our Customer Care Department within the United States at (800) 762-2974, outside the United States at (317) 572-3993 or fax (317) 572-4002.

Wiley publishes in a variety of print and electronic formats and by print-on-demand. Some material included with standard print versions of this book may not be included in e-books or in print-on-demand. If this book refers to media such as a CD or DVD that is not included in the version you purchased, you may download this material at http://booksupport.wiley.com. For more information about Wiley products, visit www.wiley.com.

A catalog record for this book is available from the Library of Congress

ISBN 9781119611042 (Paperback)
ISBN 9781119611080 (ePDF)
ISBN 9781119611066 (ePub)

Cover image: Sofie Lind Mesterton
Cover design: Thomas Madsen

Printed in the United States of America

V10014458_100519

Welcome to Visual Collaboration

Many organizations struggle to find engaging and effective communication processes to manage increasing complexity. Some attempt digital solutions and new organizational structures. Others are still searching for tools to foster the ongoing collaboration complex organizations require.

If you want to run meetings, projects, and processes that are more engaging, efficient, and impactful, this book is for you. The tools you will find here will strengthen thinking, communication, and collaboration anywhere. By using visual tools and techniques, including simple drawings that anyone can learn, Visual Collaboration can support any type of organization in managing complex projects and encouraging innovation. It will help you develop solid visual literacy skills that become foundational in your work.

If this is your first encounter with the strategic use of visuals, you are at the edge of an exciting mind-set change in how you work. If you are an experienced user of visuals, we believe the Five Building Blocks of Visual Collaboration presented in this book will give you a new and systematic approach to further develop your own visual literacy and strengthen the visual skills in the teams with whom you work.

In this book you will learn how to draw objects, people, places, processes, and more complex concepts like user experiences, business plans, and strategies. You will also learn how to design any meeting, project, or process, how to define powerful questions to engage your peers, and how to create visual templates that can focus any conversation. Finally you will learn how to scale your design so it creates a wide impact across your organization.

When people draw together, they learn together. The big picture comes into view and everyone can see themselves in it. Frontrunners such as LEGO, the UN, Maersk, IKEA, and the Red Cross have already successfully incorporated this way of working. How might you?

Contents

The five colored chapters present the Five Building Blocks of Visual Collaboration™ —a practical method for working visually. The remaining chapters offer different perspectives on visual collaboration.

INTRODUCTION

Visual Collaboration

Why a more visual way of working creates value.

CHAPTER 1	CHAPTER 2	CHAPTER 3	CHAPTER 4	CHAPTER 5
Discover your visual language	**Design your collaboration process**	**Define key questions**	**Create engaging templates**	**Prepare to scale**
How to develop icons for your next meeting, project, or process	How to create your next meeting, project, or process	How to formulate, prioritize, and test questions that have positive impact on your collaboration	How to turn a white canvas into a visual tool that structures and focuses your collaboration	How to enable others to use your design and tools

Have you ever felt stuck with methods, tools, and skills that do not match the increasing complexity you are part of?

Apply the Five Building Blocks of Visual Collaboration

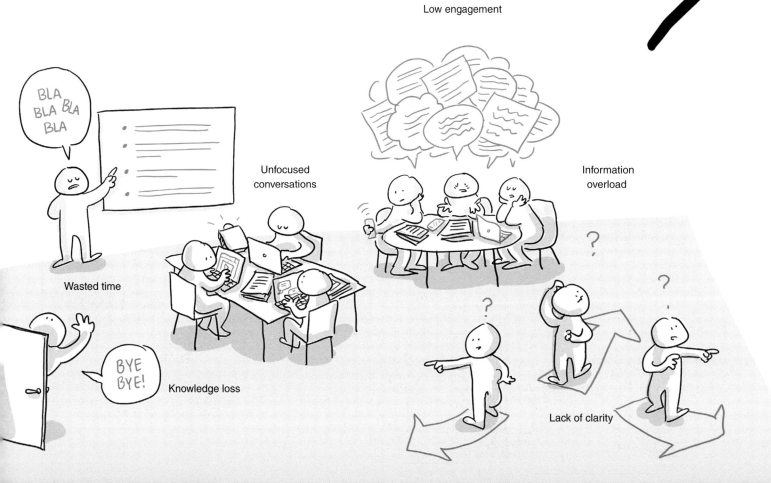

... and start working in new ways that strengthen thinking, communication and, collaboration.

Introduction

THE BOOK IN ONE PICTURE

PURPOSE: TO STRENGTHEN THE WAY YOU THINK, COMMUNICATE, AND COLLABORATE

INTRODUCTION

1 DISCOVER YOUR VISUAL LANGUAGE

2 DESIGN YOUR COLLABORATION PROCESS

3 DEFINE KEY QUESTIONS

4 CREATE ENGAGING TEMPLATES

5 PREPARE TO SCALE

THE FIVE BUILDING BLOCKS

GOAL: YOU ARE READY FOR VISUAL COLLABORATION

6 ENABLE GROUP LEARNING

7 MAP YOUR SKILLS

8 ACTIVATE YOUR RESOURCES

9 DO'S & DON'TS

13

Why draw?

Drawing is an age-old discipline that we all can learn and which the brain grasps faster than it does speech or text. When we draw, we create clarity, and in a digital world, handmade drawings stand out.

IT PROMOTES MEMORY

Drawings and images get engraved in our memory. When we only hear information, we are likely to remember 10% of it three days later. Add an image, we'll likely remember 65%. When we draw, we use that dominant power of vision to create material that our brains can better remember than speech or text.

IT HAS WORKED FOR 30,000 YEARS

As humans we were drawing long before we could write. Drawing is an age-old discipline that focuses attention and communicates volumes.

EVERYONE CAN LEARN TO DRAW

Most of us drew long before we learned to write. We can rediscover our innate potential for drawing as we create simple illustrations, and connect words with pictures. Everyone can do it.

IT CREATES CLARITY

The moment we start to draw an idea, a clarification process begins. The content of the idea is made concrete. The drawing process prompts new ideas that challenge, adjust, and refine the original understanding. The drawing product can serve as a tool to clarify understandings with others as you engage them in dialogue about the content of the drawing.

IT'S PERSONAL

Drawings are unique creations that stand out as personal and authentic, especially in a digital world.

IT ACTIVATES IMAGINATION

Imagine that you've won a trip to your dream destination. Who is joining you? Where are you headed? And what will you do there? By drawing you can quickly show others how you envision the future, and together you can grasp, discuss, and shape it.

Who can draw and where?

Everyone can use drawing as an effective tool for communication. Technology has given us new means to draw, adjust, and share our drawings with one another.

ANYONE CAN USE IT

Regardless of role or function, we can all enjoy drawing and benefit from using it.

IN ANY SITUATION

Dare to draw in your next meeting, workshop, or conference. It will bring a fresh perspective.

ON ANY SURFACE

Most meeting facilities have a whiteboard or a rolling flip chart. If you can draw on paper, you can also draw on a whiteboard with the right markers. Working with digital interfaces is slightly different. If you are a computer fan, find a good drawing program you like. Computer drawing makes it easy to adjust your drawings and share them with colleagues.

THE NEED IS GROWING

Our sharing of knowledge and information has exploded. Our social structures and patterns are often described as hypercomplex. The need for tools to navigate this complexity is growing. When we structure knowledge and information in visual phrases and build a visual language for a specific context, we create frameworks that advance our understanding of the complex systems in which we must act. It helps us see the bigger picture and make decisions accordingly.

TECHNOLOGY MAKES IT EASILY SCALABLE

The last 30 years have seen astonishing technological developments with respect to using, sharing, and navigating visual materials. Opportunities for working visually are already in place in a wide range of readily available apps and programs. With a visually oriented younger generation, that range of visual platforms will continue to expand.

Why draw together?

To see the bigger picture, we need a greater knowledge base than we see on our own. Visual collaboration is when we draw together to learn from other perspectives and build shared responsibility and ownership. Drawing together can create a common language across cultures, positions, and national borders.

COMPLEX CHALLENGES ARE NOT SOLVED IN ISOLATION

Drawing together is a systematic approach to complexity management. When we draw together, we work with a broader vision and base of knowledge. We can create more complete views of the whole and clarify connections and similarities and differences in understanding. Developing a shared drawing is an iterative process. We draw, stop, and jointly observe what we have created, and then draw more. This process trains our view of the whole, because we see one another's contributions in a shared context. This builds a common understanding of the bigger picture.

IT'S ENGAGING

Many meetings fail to engage more than a few participants. When we draw together, we relate to space differently. We move more. We reshuffle group dynamics and hierarchies as a new discipline is put into play. We practice constructive risk taking. We communicate more. Creative expression puts a smile on people's faces while energizing their participation.

IT CREATES OWNERSHIP

People who contribute to something have a greater sense of ownership. Each individual contributor who helps create a shared drawing has tangible evidence of their contribution and can see their own contributions as part of a bigger whole. This enhances commitment.

IT'S EASY TO SHARE

When you have been involved in developing a visualization of a strategy or project, you know it inside and out. You can represent the drawing and its narrative to others who have not been involved. The drawing can serve as a collective learning tool that is easy to share with others.

IT CREATES A COMMON LANGUAGE

Having a common visual language strengthens communication around a given topic. We can share understandings and make sure that we are talking about the same thing. A commonly understood visual language can support a high level of complexity in our conversations.

Vocabulary for Visual Collaboration

Visual Collaboration is a guidebook for working more visually in meetings, projects, and processes. These three terms are good to know:

Facilitation enables a group to work together effectively and therefore make better decisions.
Good facilitators can:
– Put themselves in someone else's place.
– Create a shared sense of identity in a group.
– Energize a group and engage it in the service of a stated purpose.
– Find, formulate, and ask good questions.
– Listen actively and with focus.

Visual facilitation is facilitation with structured use of pen and paper.

The concept of visual facilitation stems from the concept of graphic facilitation, which was formulated in the 1970s by a group of organizational consultants in California who used visual techniques and tools to find solutions to complex issues.

Visual facilitation uses visual representations to facilitate interaction in a group of people, using structured visual content. It is a systematic way of drawing together with others.

A good visual facilitator can capture communication in handwritten text so content is accessible to the group being facilitated. A good visual facilitator can translate the content of a process into drawings that are informative, straightforward, and comprehensive.

Visual facilitation can be as basic as facilitating a process by means of simple visual tools, like a few color-coded sticky notes, and a well-formulated question.

System visualization is a concept for visual collaboration. Through the lens of systems theory, we observe and structure knowledge visually.

Inspired by a wide range of front-runners in visualization, design thinking, change theory, facilitation, process management, and systems theory, as well as our own experience, we have developed the practical method of this book: the Five Building Blocks of Visual Collaboration. Each building block supports the overall purpose of system visualization: to facilitate communication and systems understanding in a group through targeted questions and visual representations to achieve valuable results.

Visual collaboration is also when...

...you and your colleagues stand in front of a flip chart and fill out sticky notes with ideas or tasks that you post and arrange in groups.

...you explain an idea or a concept by visualizing it.

...you work with others to create a mind map of an important topic or project.

… you and your project team chart a process by drawing it in broad strokes and then filling in each part of the process together.

… you use visual tools in your weekly meetings to update one another about various projects.

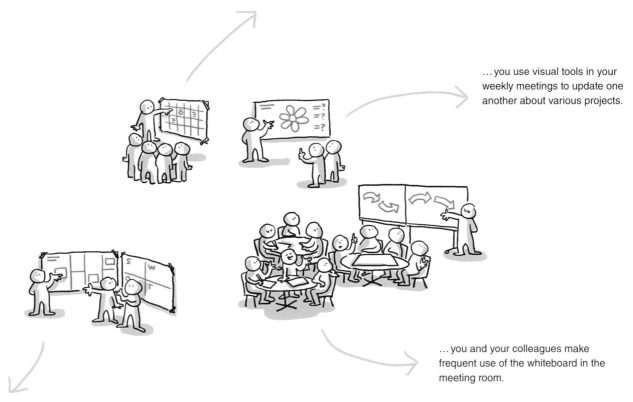

… you and your colleagues make frequent use of the whiteboard in the meeting room.

… you and your colleagues create a SWOT analysis with strengths, weaknesses, opportunities, and threats.

Boost your visual literacy

To gain the benefits of visual collaboration, here is a way to
quickly get skilled at drawing.

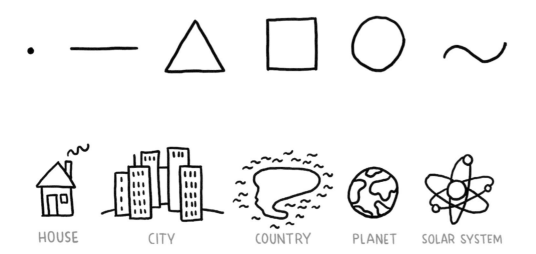

HOUSE   CITY   COUNTRY   PLANET   SOLAR SYSTEM

You just need to practice combining basic
shapes. With a dot, a line, a triangle, a square, a
circle, and a wave you can draw a house, a town,
a country, a planet, or an entire solar system.

Drawing with basic shapes is an easy, rapid,
and intuitive way of visualizing.

You only need to draw a fraction of what the eye sees to create recognition and understanding. Start seeing the world through a lense of basic shapes, practice drawing easy objects, and expand your visual vocabulary along the way.

From basic shapes to icons

Think of a word you want to represent visually and draw it as simply as you can.

From icons to templates

Make simple visual templates with the icons you create.

SHOW THE AGENDA OF
YOUR MEETING

MAP THE COMPETENCIES
OF YOUR TEAM

**GET EVERYONE ON THE SAME PAGE WITH
A PROCESS OVERVIEW**

**BRAINSTORM AND
PRIORITIZE IDEAS**

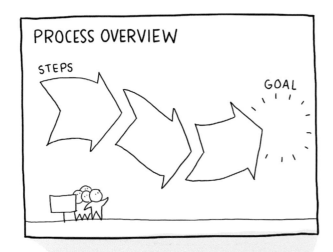

The Five Building Blocks of Visual Collaboration™

The five building blocks constitute a systematic method to develop and reinforce your approach to visual work.

Each building block guides you step-by-step through a given process and also provides templates, models, question lists, and training guides that you can use and customize to your needs. Learning the Five Building Blocks of Visual Collaboration will provide you with simple tools and techniques for visual collaboration.

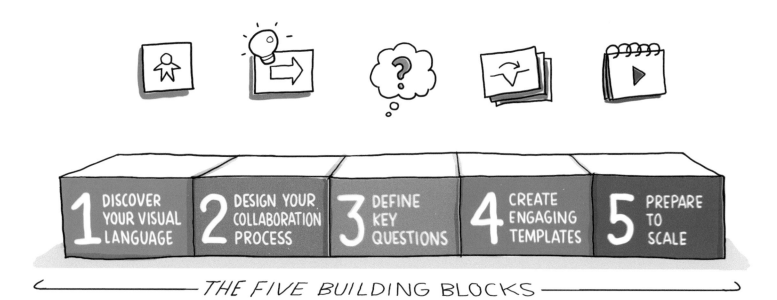

THE FIVE BUILDING BLOCKS

How to use the building blocks

Work with all five building blocks in sequence.

Or start with a building block that fits a specific need.

The Five Building Blocks are designed to create value as a whole. Start with building block one and work your way through all five when you want the full benefit of visual collaboration.

Start with block one if you need a visual language for a given topic.

Jump to block two if you want to think through a meeting or workshop.

Dive deep with block three if you want to explore questions for a conversation.

Go to block four if you just need inspiration for how to create a template for a specific training.

A meeting needs to be planned and facilitated.

Create a visual language for the topic of your meeting.

Visually think through your meeting.

Categorize, prioritize, and test questions to use in your meeting.

Design a visual template for your meeting.

Use block five if you are
all set with a process
and want to make others
able to follow it.

Develope a visual playbook that
guides how others can facilitate
your meeting.

You are ready.

You run a focused and
engaging meeting.

Your design creates
value beyond your
initial meeting.

Using the building blocks for a strategy process

Throughout the book you will meet this example: An executive team wants to engage their entire organization in strategic conversations. Three managers are handed the task to plan and facilitate the process, first as a workshop for the top management, and later as a series of workshops held throughout the organization.

Task received.

1

The team creates a visual langauge for strategy.

2

They visually think through the strategy workshop.

3

Key questions for the strategy workshop are listed, categorized, prioritized, and tested.

4

The team designs a visual tool to focus the conversations at the workshop.

They develop a visual playbook enabling others to facilitate the strategy workshop.

The team is ready.

They run and facilitate the workshop.

The workshop concept is rolled out across the organization.

Summary

Visual Collaboration: Using visuals when collaborating can bring the bigger picture into view and build shared language, ownership, and commitment in a group dealing with complex challenges.

Three terms that are good to know:

- *Facilitation* enables a group to work together effectively.
- *Visual facilitation* is facilitation with structured use of pen and paper.
- *System visualization* is used to facilitate communication and systems understanding in a group through targeted questions and visual representations to achieve valuable results.

The Five Building Blocks of Visual Collaboration:
A practical method for visual facilitation. The method for visual collaboration is based on system visualization and is built on five distinct building blocks:

1. Discover your visual language.
2. Design your collaboration process.
3. Define key questions.
4. Create engaging templates.
5. Prepare to scale.

WHAT WAS YOUR LATEST DRAWING?

1.
Discover your visual language

DISCOVER YOUR VISUAL LANGUAGE

PURPOSE: TO SHOW HOW YOU CAN DRAW (ALMOST) ANYTHING

GOAL: YOU HAVE A VISUAL LANGUAGE FOR YOUR NEXT MEETING, PROJECT, OR PROCESS

TOOL: ICON DESIGNER
PAGE 66

EXAMPLES
PAGE 68

6 ENABLE GROUP LEARNING

7 MAP YOUR SKILLS

8 ACTIVATE YOUR RESOURCES

9 DO'S & DON'TS

The Seven Elements™

A shortcut to a visual language

Every meeting involves a group of people in a given place, at a given time, to discuss a given subject.

If we translate this formula into a visual alphabet, we can build a visual language to use in meetings and processes. We call this the Seven Elements.

Practice drawing each element as you read through this chapter.

1. People

2. Places

3. Processes 4. Speech 5. Text 6. Color 7. Effects

THE SEVEN ELEMENTS

1. People

Show who is involved. We all like to see ourselves represented. We want to know where we fit in, who else is involved, and what roles and responsibilities belong to whom.

For drawing people, find a style that is easy for you to draw and easy for others to decipher. Most people are familiar with stick figures.

Try drawing a star figure too. It has volume and you can readily adapt it to indicate movement, dress, and attitude. By coloring it, you can show different roles, responsibilities, or profiles in a process.

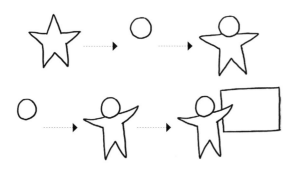

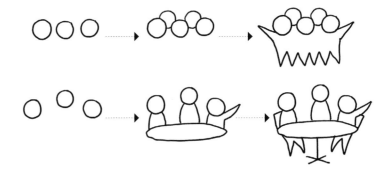

DRAW STARS

Practice drawing five-pointed stars.
Replace the top point with a circle.

DUPLICATE

Draw a lot of circles and points. It can be important to count heads when drawing a group, but less important to count arms and legs.

EXPERIMENT

Let arms and legs point in different directions as a way of showing movement and mood.

THE SEVEN ELEMENTS

2. Places

Show how and when. We orient ourselves in time and place. We want to be able to see where we are and when.

Keep the place drawing simple. Use signs, labels, and platforms to indicate time and place.

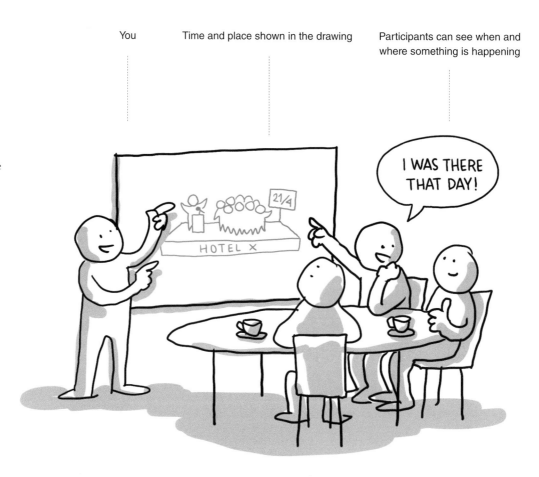

You

Time and place shown in the drawing

Participants can see when and where something is happening

I WAS THERE THAT DAY!

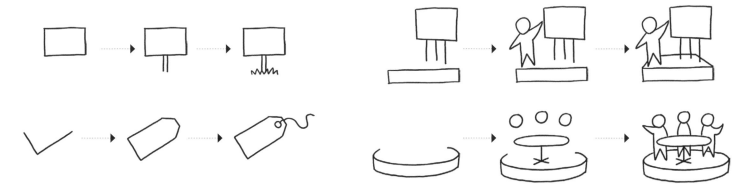

SIGNS AND LABELS

Frame important information by placing signs and labels on your drawing.

PLATFORMS

Show time and place by drawing a platform for your situation. Give it volume, so it has room for text or color.

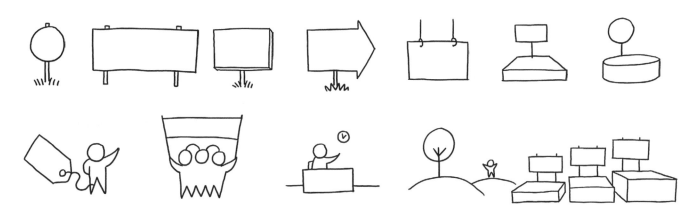

SHAPES

Vary the shapes on your signs and platforms when you want to highlight content differently.

HORIZON LINES

A horizontal line indicates that one is indoors, an arched line that one is outside.

THE SEVEN ELEMENTS

3. Processes

Show sequence, direction, and context. It is often important to show where one is in a sequence and indicate direction or show connections.

Use arrows to show process and sharpen understanding of a sequence. Arrows can also show relationships between people and units.

Show systems, or how communication, information, and decisions move in your organization.

48

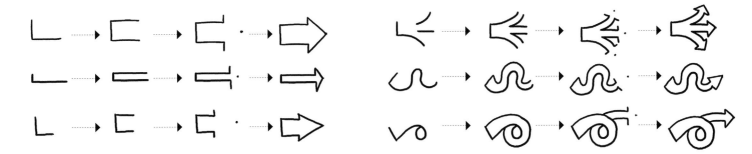

DRAW IN STAGES

First draw the body of the arrow. Then draw the arms of the arrow, and then a dot in the middle of the arrow's body. Finally, draw the tip of the arrow.

DIFFERENTIATE

Create long or short arrow bodies, angles, and tips. Create different arrows, so your processes can be differentiated from one another.

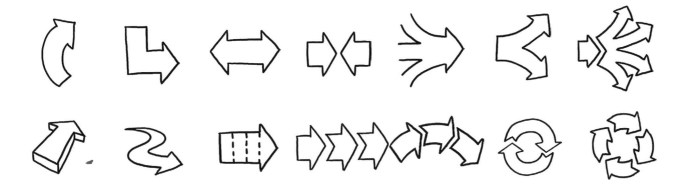

EXPERIMENT

Arrows can take many forms. Experiment and combine different shapes of arrowheads until you find what fits your process.

THE SEVEN ELEMENTS

4. Speech

Show statements, thoughts, and feelings. These bring the drawing to life. You can show your participants that you heard what they said. You can also open a dialogue about the unsaid—about thoughts and feelings.

Speech or thought bubbles can look very different. Their shape can be used to express agreement, disagreement, frustration, happiness, and many other feelings.

50

DRAW CIRCLES

Practice drawing circles. Pivot the pen quickly so the circle does not become uneven. Make a circle with an opening to add a "tail."

START WITH THE TEXT

Always write the content of your thought bubble first. Then draw the frame and finally the "tail."

EXPERIMENT

Dig your old comic books out of storage and let yourself be inspired!

THE SEVEN ELEMENTS

5. Text

Show context. A combination of text and drawing sharpens the content and clarifies meaning.

Underpin your drawings with strong headings, descriptive messages, and carefully selected citations.

Take some time on text selection so you only write the essentials into your drawing.

Practice writing clearly so your text can easily be read, even at a distance.

| You | Headings, words, and phrases in the drawing | The participants can read the most important content |

UNCLEAR TEXT

CLEAR TEXT

Lower case letters for quotations and longer sections of text.

WRITE CLEARLY

Allow the lines to meet so each letter appears as a clear and single shape. Leave clear spaces.

GRIDLINES HELP

USE GRIDLINES

Create gridlines with light colors and write the letters perpendicularly on the line. Experiment with various forms of grid lines.

HEADING 1

- **HEADING 2**

  → HEADING 3
  →
  →

CREATE LEVELS

Use bulleted lists and texts of different sizes to show informational hierarchy.

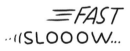

USE VARIETY

Give your heading shading or change text size when you want to show connection or difference.

THE SEVEN ELEMENTS

6. Color

Show relations, differences, and similarities. Using color strategically will help your participants see relationships, differences, and similarities.

You work strategically with colors when, for example, you use only green sticky notes for actions in a process and only blue ones for role descriptions. Do this in your drawings as well. Use color codes to organize input from your participants, categorize systems, or show different employee groups.

54

**DARK TEXT
EASY TO READ**
GOOD CONTRAST
CLEAR

GOOD FOR CONTOURS:

DIFFICULT TO
READ, BETTER FOR
UNDERLYING
FRAMING

HIGHLIGHT
ADD COLOR:

DARK COLORS

Dark colors on white paper create clear contrast that makes the text easy to read. This is particularly important on a whiteboard, where there can be glare.

LIGHT COLORS

Light colors are more difficult to read on a white background, but light colors are good for underlining, highlighting, and coloring.

HEADING

USE COLOR CODES

Help the eye navigate around the content of the drawing by using specific colors consistently.

THE SEVEN ELEMENTS

7. Effects

Show energy, movement, and depth. Effects can create life and understanding.

A little line or a dot can make all the difference for your drawing.

If your star figure has arms over its head and dashes in a circle from hand to hand, you are showing happiness; if your figure has its shoulders hunched up to its ears and a black zigzag line over its head, you're indicating frustration.

Use simple lines and shapes to emphasize meaning.

You   Effects used in the drawing   Participants can see energy, movement, and depth

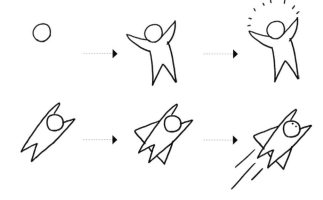 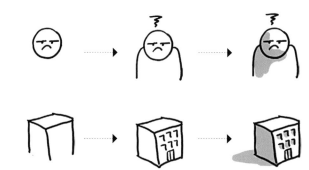

ENERGY LINES

With a few energy lines you can add energy to the objects and people you draw.

MOVEMENT LINES

Lines placed before, after, or below an object can indicate motion or position.

FEELING LINES

Clarify feelings with a few extra lines.

SHADING

Draw a thick gray line next to or below an object. This adds depth and perspective.

The Seven Elements combined

Show things as a whole. The Seven Elements jointly form a visual alphabet. Use all seven elements when you are designing templates for presentations or dialogues. Make the alphabet your own.

Practice: Take an 11" × 17" sheet of paper and create an overview picture step-by-step. Start by dividing your sheet into nine equally sized fields with two vertical and two horizontal light gray gridlines. This makes it easier to compose your drawing. The example to the right shows the structure of a path through training.

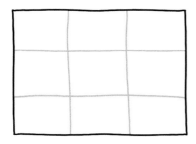

Grid lines

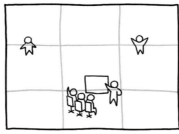

1. People

2. Places

3. Processes

4. Speech

5. Text

6. Color

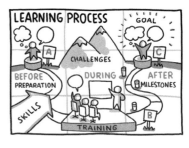

7. Effects

 Scan the code and watch the training video
"The Seven Elements."

The Eighth Element™

Expand your visual vocabulary

When working visually, it is valuable to have a large visual vocabulary—a visual language—that can always be further enlarged and shaped by the projects and processes you are a part of.

If you wish to build a visual language for a project, you can use the method the Eighth Element.

– *List* the most important words in the project.
– *Categorize* words into things, places, people, processes, and concepts.
– *Design* icons by visualizing, simplifying, combining, and deciding on their meaning.

Where applicable, use the Icon Designer to get an overview and further develop the visual language of your project.

List

Categorize

60

Design

THE EIGHTH ELEMENT

List

List the most important words. List the most important words and terms describing projects, processes, and the areas you work with.

Think of one of your projects and list all the words and concepts for which it might make sense to have icons.

One group works with strategy and lists their most important words

Categorizing things, people, and places in a project helps you to visualize the words you have categorized under processes and concepts.

Categorize

Categorize your words. When you categorize things, people, places, processes, and concepts, you are forced to "see" your words. You must decide whether a word describes, for example, a physical object, or if it instead describes a process. You begin visualizing the words as soon as you start categorizing them.

THE EIGHTH ELEMENT

Design

Visualize, simplify, combine, and decide. In this step you will develop your icons. Start with words from concrete categories (things, people, places). These are often the easiest. Move on to abstract words (processes and concepts). Take one word at a time, and ask yourself: "What does this word look like?" Use the basic shapes and the Seven Elements, and design icons by visualizing, simplifying, combining, and deciding on their meaning.

VISUALIZE

Imagine your word. Use your mind's eye to see what your words refer to in the real world. What does your word describe? What do you see when you think of the word? What things or people are included? What is surrounding your word? Where does it take place? If you viewed the word through a camera lens, what would the photo you take depict?

SIMPLIFY

Keep it simple. Remove all superfluous information and all ambiguity. Your icon should be easy for others in your project to understand, use, and copy. It should be easy to draw—preferably with ten strokes or less.

COMBINE

Put your icons together. Experiment with different combinations of icons, and see how new meaning arises. If you are working with words from the abstract categories, it can often make sense to combine them with icons from the concrete categories.

DECIDE

Decide on their meaning. All icons can be interpreted differently, depending on who is viewing or using them. Emphasize the meaning of your icon by writing its word below the drawing. An icon is not static. It is when you use the icon that meaning is ascribed.

 Scan the code and watch the training video "The Eighth Element."

Icon Designer

HOW

Download or create the Icon Designer. This is a template with a large table. You work with the tool from the bottom to the top, following the steps list, categorize, and design. The three steps and arrangement of icons and words make it easy to combine, refine, and develop your visual language. Use sticky notes so your tool is flexible.

STICKY NOTES

Use square sticky notes for your icons.

→ *Drawing*

→ *Denominator*

Use rectangular sticky notes when you are listing words.

 Download the Icon Designer on
www.visualcollaboration.site.

ICON DESIGNER

VISUAL LANGUAGE FOR: _____

DATE: _____

BY: _____

	THINGS	PEOPLE	PLACES	PROCESSES	CONCEPTS
DESIGN:					
CATEGORIZE:					

LIST:

TOOL   EXAMPLE

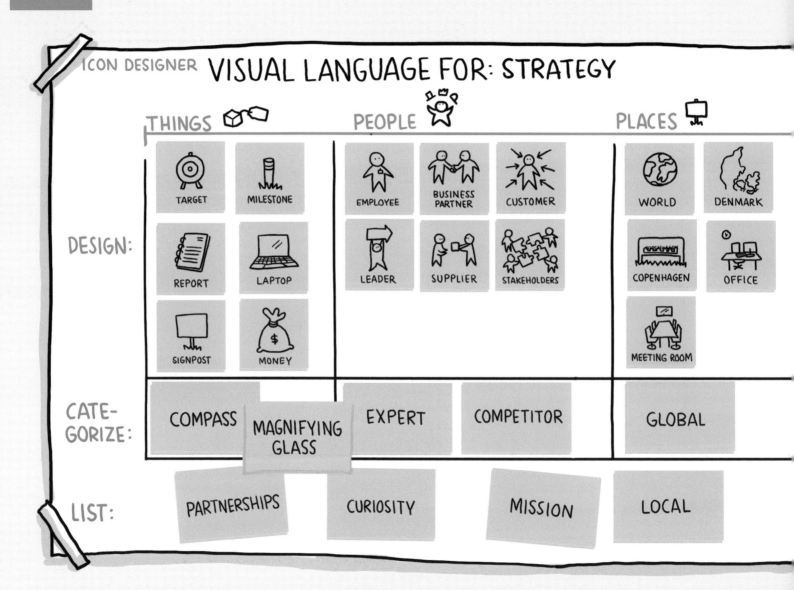

ICON DESIGNER   VISUAL LANGUAGE FOR: STRATEGY

THINGS   PEOPLE   PLACES

DESIGN:

THINGS: TARGET, MILESTONE, REPORT, LAPTOP, SIGNPOST, MONEY

PEOPLE: EMPLOYEE, BUSINESS PARTNER, CUSTOMER, LEADER, SUPPLIER, STAKEHOLDERS

PLACES: WORLD, DENMARK, COPENHAGEN, OFFICE, MEETING ROOM

CATE-GORIZE: COMPASS, MAGNIFYING GLASS, EXPERT, COMPETITOR, GLOBAL

LIST: PARTNERSHIPS, CURIOSITY, MISSION, LOCAL

PROCESSES

 LEADING
 DEVELOP
 ATTRACT
 ANALYZE

 GROW
 CHANGE
 MEASURE
 PRIORITIZE

 COLLABORATION

CONCEPTS

 DIVERSITY
 TREND
VISION

 CHALLENGE
 THREAT
 IDEA
 STRATEGY

 STRENGTHS
 WEAKNESSES

EVALUATE LEARN

INNOVATION INITIATIVE

RECRUITMENT DECISION ALTERNATIVES

ICON DESIGNER   VISUAL LANGUAGE FOR: CLIMATE CHANGE

THINGS   PEOPLE   PLACES

DESIGN:

THINGS		PEOPLE			PLACES	
SPROUT	CAR	INDIVIDUAL	FAMILY	REFUGEE	HOME	FOREST
WINDMILL	GREENHOUSE GASES	WORKER	POLITICIAN	DELEGATION	FACTORY	EARTH
TREE	NATIONAL FLAG				METROPOLIS	MINISTRY

CATE-GORIZE:

WASTE	RESEARCHER EXPERT	VILLAGE

LIST:

LIFESTYLE   EXPOSED COMMUNITIES   RAIN FOREST   ADAPTION

PROCESSES

 CO_2 REDUCTION	FLOODING	NEGOTIATION	REFORESTATION
COLLABORATION	RECYCLING	DEVELOPMENT	OIL DRILLING
DROUGHT			

CONCEPTS

GREEN TECHNOLOGY	GREEN JOBS	OVERPOPULATION	CLIMATE REFUGEES
CO_2 NEUTRAL	WATER POLLUTION	NATURAL DISASTERS	RISK
CONSENSUS	RESPONSIBILITY		

MIGRATE	MEASURE		MEDIA	FINANCIAL SECTOR

SUSTAINABLE	SOLAR ENERGY	SCEPTICS

Summary

The Seven Elements is a system to create a visual language for meetings, processes, and projects, whatever their content. Combine the Seven Elements into wholes that are relevant for you.

The Eighth Element expands your visual vocabulary, creating icons specific to your context.

The Icon Designer can help you create a visual language for your project or area of work by listing, categorizing, and designing.

WHAT WORDS ARE IMPORTANT
FOR YOU, YOUR PROJECT,
OR YOUR ORGANIZATION?

WHAT DO THEY LOOK LIKE?

A visual language for innovation

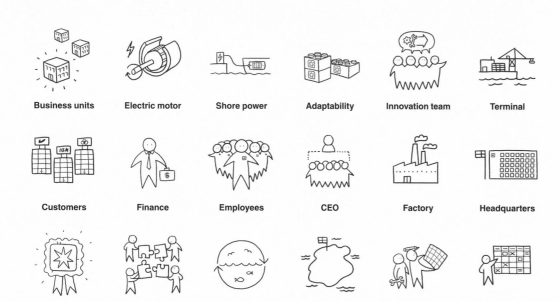

Business units	Electric motor	Shore power	Adaptability	Innovation team	Terminal
Customers	Finance	Employees	CEO	Factory	Headquarters
Reliability	Collaboration	Environment	Country	Prototyping	Project management

Example: A sample of the department's visual language, 18 icons showing the context that Technical Innovation works with.

Technical Innovation is the name of the department at A.P. Moller—Maersk that works with innovation of the technical segment of the business.

Through idea development, testing, validation, and pilot projects, they develop solutions for tomorrow's transport and logistics. And to create relevant solutions customized to the needs of the organization, the department runs processes with both internal and external teams.

Technical Innovation has developed a visual language for these processes. It is used to show others who they are, how they work, the context in which they operate, and the future that they wish to shape.

The visual language consists of 152 words with associated visualizations. It was created by employees in the department and continues to develop as new words, terms, and concepts arise.

The language is used to explain complexity and make abstract concepts more concrete.

Taking the visual language as a starting point, the department has also developed visual presentation and dialogue tools that they use when new business partners are invited in to get a grasp of and find their way through the department's innovation processes.

"When you want to create new ideas and innovate in your organization, you need to be able to engage people broadly and involve them in a different type of conversation. If you wish to create an innovation culture, you need to do things differently. You need to explore new paths, use new tools, and employ new skills. Our visualizations help us to engage other units and to explain what it is that we are doing."

Julija Voitiekute
Innovation Portfolio Manager—Technical Innovation, A.P. Moller—Maersk

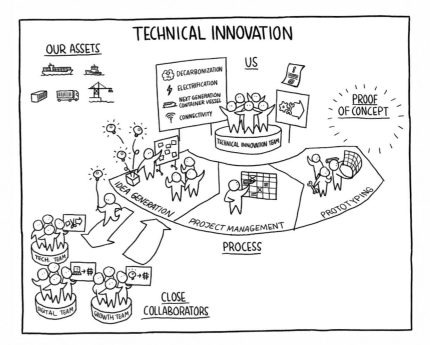

Example: A presentation tool showing one of Technical Innovation's working methods.

Example: "Energy Harvest"
The icon shows the ship of the future utilizing natural sources of energy.

2.
Design your collaboration process

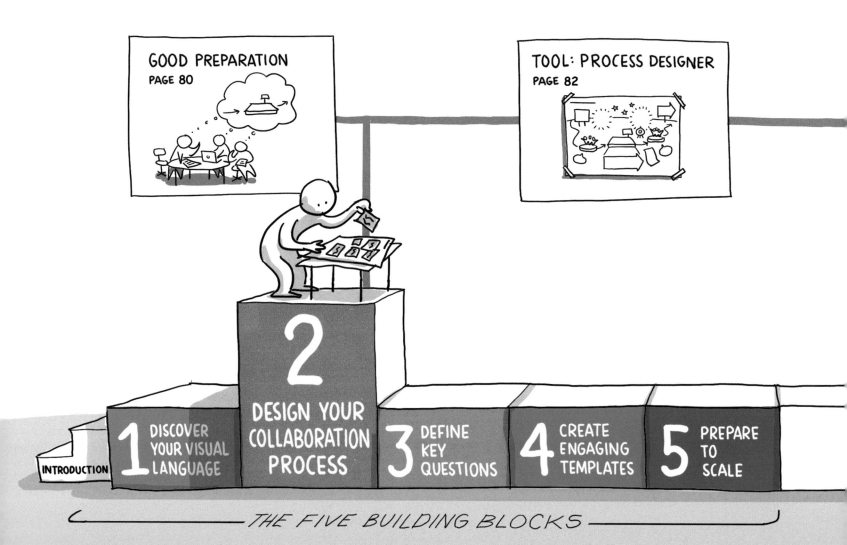

GOAL: YOU ARE READY TO SUCCESSFULLY RUN YOUR NEXT MEETING, PROJECT, OR PROCESS

HOW TO USE THE TOOL
PAGE 94

EXAMPLES
PAGE 96

6 ENABLE GROUP LEARNING

7 MAP YOUR SKILLS

8 ACTIVATE YOUR RESOURCES

9 DO'S & DON'TS

Good preparation

Behind any good process you will usually find good preparation.
Preparing well for a process you want to facilitate will create a strong
starting point for engaging participants and achieving good results.
These ten process questions can help you and your colleagues do that.

Remember: Start with background and
purpose. Once the purpose is formulated,
the answers to the remaining questions
come easier. Work with them in whatever
sequence works best for the process.

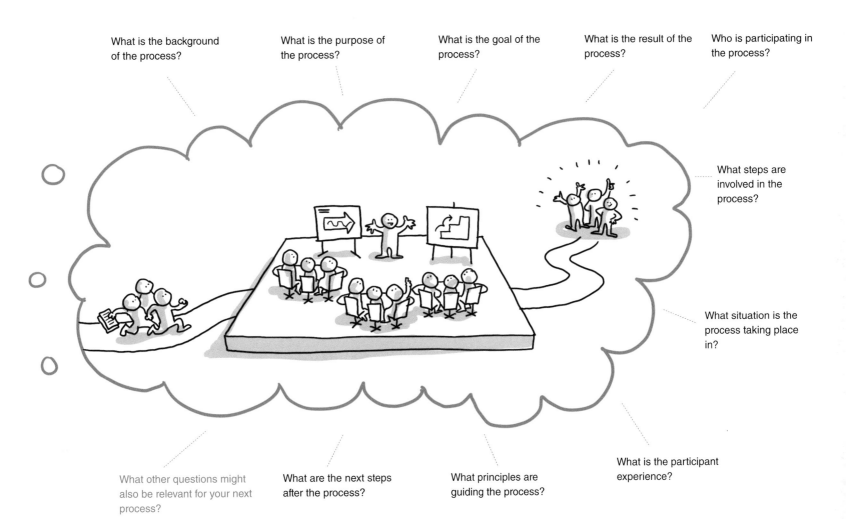

What is the background of the process?

What is the purpose of the process?

What is the goal of the process?

What is the result of the process?

Who is participating in the process?

What steps are involved in the process?

What situation is the process taking place in?

What other questions might also be relevant for your next process?

What are the next steps after the process?

What principles are guiding the process?

What is the participant experience?

Process Designer

Use the Process Designer to achieve a focused dialogue with your colleagues about your upcoming process. Discover new connections, see blind spots, and create the whole together.

On the template each of the ten process questions is represented by an icon, and they jointly make up a visual narrative of your entire upcoming process.

STRUCTURE OF THE TEMPLATE

The background of the process is placed on the horizon to the left. Next to this, raised up in the air, there is a place to write the *purpose* of the process. On the right side of the template you find space for the process *goal*, which has a target as an icon. Below the target there is a document with room to list the process *results*.

   Process participants are drawn into the template in two places —on the path to the right and the path to the left. The *participant experience* before the process is entered on the left. Participant experience after the process is entered on the right.

   The platform in the middle of the template symbolizes the *situation*, i.e., the process itself. A few stars are hanging over the platform. These symbolize *the principles* that will guide the process. Below the platform there is an arrow that shows *the process steps*.

   At the top right corner an arrow sign with a pair of footprints is drawn, where you can fill in the *next steps* of the process.

HOW?

Draw the template or download as a PDF. The number of participants, process steps, and situation content can be adjusted in relation to the current process.

Download the Process Designer on
www.visualcollaboration.site.

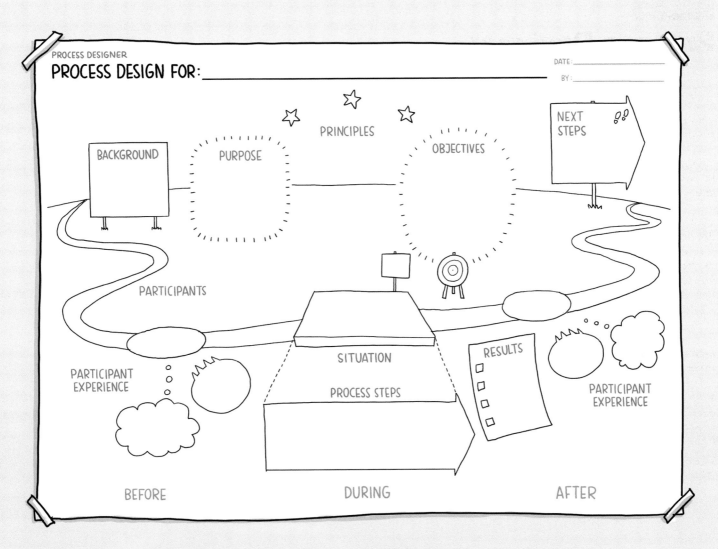

PROCESS DESIGNER

PROCESS DESIGN FOR:_____

DATE:_____

BY:_____

PRINCIPLES

BACKGROUND

PURPOSE

OBJECTIVES

NEXT STEPS

PARTICIPANTS

PARTICIPANT EXPERIENCE

SITUATION

RESULTS

PROCESS STEPS

PARTICIPANT EXPERIENCE

BEFORE

DURING

AFTER

PROCESS DESIGNER

Background

What is the background?
The background field describes what came before the process—in other words, the reason the process was launched.

The most essential needs, trends, events, data, or decisions that have led to the desire to launch the process are listed here.

EXAMPLE

Manager prepares a presentation for his or her employees.

CONSIDERATIONS

What has led to me having to do this presentation? What needs did it arise from? What events, decisions, or data serve as the basis for the presentation?

Purpose

What is the purpose of the process?
A purpose provides an answer as to *why* a process should unfold.

A clear purpose is meaningful and focused. Each activity and each result of a process must be able to be evaluated in relation to the purpose of the process.

The purpose must be convincing, and it must be able to guide the participants toward the desired result.

EXAMPLE

Employees are preparing a new structure for their department's weekly meeting.

CONSIDERATIONS

Why have the participants come together? What is the purpose of their weekly meetings?

85

PROCESS DESIGNER

Goal

What is the goal of the process?
A goal describes what one wishes to achieve.

The goal sets the direction. Every process should have a clear and well-described goal that can provide participants with energy and inspire a desire to contribute.

It is easier to move in the direction of concrete goals. A well-formulated goal can be used throughout the process to assess whether you are on the right track.

EXAMPLE

A project group is designing a management seminar.

CONSIDERATIONS

What is the goal of the management seminar? What should we aim for? How can we see that we have reached the goal? How do our goal and our purpose coincide?

THE MANAGERS UNDERSTAND THEIR NEW ROLES, TASKS, AND RESPONSIBILITIES

Results

What is the result of the process?
Concrete results can be seen, weighed, measured, and counted. Articulating process results makes the process goal action-oriented. What needs to come out of the process is made clear. Beyond the process it is not the goal, but rather the results, that are taken on further.

The results must correspond with the purpose and goal of the process.

EXAMPLE

The innovation team is planning an idea-generation workshop.

CONSIDERATIONS

What results are to be generated by the workshop? What concrete elements shall be produced during the course of the workshop? What visible and measurable results show that we have reached the goal?

PROCESS DESIGNER

Participants

Who is participating in the process? The individuals participating in the process are described in the participants field. They can be described with different profiles—needs, interests, roles, responsibilities, and tasks—or as a collective group with common characteristics.

It is important to clarify what type of participant will be involved, so that all are involved in the best possible way, and to ensure that everyone can help support the purpose of the process.

For all participants or participant groups, a brief description is given of who they are, where they come from, and what they will be contributing.

EXAMPLE

A training session is being prepared.

CONSIDERATIONS

Who are the participants? What is their interest in the training session? Who holds what roles, responsibilities, and tasks along the way? What characterizes the participants as a group? What resources does each individual participant have, and how are these put into play?

88

Principles

What principles are guiding the process?
Principles are guidelines or guiding stars that describe how we best work together in a given process.

Principles express attitudes, values, and qualities. Principles help in tackling the challenges that can arise along the way in a process.

A principle needs to allow for space so it can be inclusive and not exclusive. At the same time it should be kept simple so it can be understood and owned by everyone.

EXAMPLE

A project group plans a public meeting.

CONSIDERATIONS

How should the participants collaborate in order to have worthwhile dialogue? How should the participants act to reach the goals and the desired results?

PROCESS DESIGNER

Situation

Where and when is the process taking place? This field describes the situation and the time, place, and physical context in which the process will happen: where (location), when (periods, dates, and times), and what resources are necessary (facilities, equipment, and materials)?

A good process design has a detailed situation description, so the physical surroundings support the planned process as optimally as possible.

If applicable, sketch the most ideal layout of the premises. What equipment would be needed to succeed, and what materials would be needed to work with?

EXAMPLE

A group is preparing a workshop.

CONSIDERATIONS

When is the workshop taking place? Where is it taking place? What location and what premises? What equipment and what materials will we need?

Process steps

What steps are involved in the process?
This field contains a description of the steps that make up the process from start to finish. The process steps are the building blocks that ensure that the purpose of the process unfolds within concrete activities so that the goal is reached and the results are created.

Each step in the process should have a title and a brief description. A process step can also describe who is responsible for what and when. In the first round it is only the overarching steps that need to be included in your process designer. The level of detail can be increased later in a playbook.

EXAMPLE

A group is designing an evaluation process.

CONSIDERATIONS

What process steps should the evaluation process consist of? What should we do first, along the way, and last? How is there variation in our process?

PROCESS DESIGNER

Participant experience

What participant experience does the process provide? The participant experience is a matter of putting oneself in the participants' place and formulating what the participants will experience before, during, and after a process.

Putting oneself in the participants' place is a determining factor as to whether one is successful in designing a process that is relevant. A process designer is wise to take into consideration the participants' needs, interests, and expectations of a process.

Put words and images to what the various participants think, say, and do before, during, and after the process.

EXAMPLE

A manager is preparing the employee annual review.

CONSIDERATIONS

What experience should the employee have of the meeting? What does he or she say before, during, and after the meeting? What is he or she able to do after the meeting?

92

PROCESS DESIGNER

Next step

What happens after the process? Having a clear idea of what happens immediately after a process helps ensure that the work and input that all participants add to the process are recognized. Describe follow-up in the most concrete terms possible. This can be as simple as listing who keeps the minutes or sending out a new meeting invitation. Having a clear idea of what happens immediately after a process helps ensure that the work is carried onward.

EXAMPLE

A project group is designing a conference.

CONSIDERATIONS

What happens right after the conference? Who will use the results? When and how will they be used?

How to use the tool

Use the Process Designer when designing processes—preferably together with others. The Process Designer provides a framework for your process so it is easier to chart, discuss, and design all elements, so they fit in as a whole. Allocate time, prepare, and work your way through the tool in a structured way.

1. DRAW

Draw a large version of the tool so you and your colleagues can stand in front of it and work. If applicable, download it as a PDF in A0 to print as a poster or as standard copy-paper size, with instructions included in the drawing.

2. BRAINSTORM

Go through all the process questions one by one. What are the angles on each question? What are possible answers? Are all stakeholders and participants accounted for? Start broadly, write all answers down on sticky notes, and set them up in the corresponding fields on the tool. Where is there agreement? Where are the answers far apart from one another? The number of sticky notes for each of the individual questions can indicate where more work should be carried out with that content.

3. GROUP

Look through all the sticky notes question by question and group them by common denominator. Some groups may have a lot of sticky notes, others few. Do new ideas come up? Can you chart patterns? Discuss what characterizes each group.

94

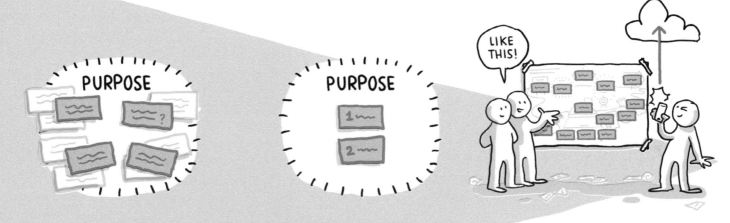

4. FORMULATE

Take a step back and look at the answers to each question. How can you formulate a new heading that captures the most important points? Write the headings on new sticky notes. Use short sentences so they are easy to remember. Prioritize your sticky notes and keep only the best ones.

5. SELECT

What is the crux of what you want to get out of the process? How can this best be expressed in your answers? How can you focus and simplify? Create a prioritized sequence of all the answers to each question. Select the one or two most important answers, and keep them in this field or write/draw them into the tool. Remove the remaining sticky notes.

6. DOCUMENT AND SHARE

Once you have gone through all ten questions in this manner, you have a comprehensive process design. Take a picture of the results, share it with everyone involved, and use it in the next stages of work to document the process, and, if applicable, in communication with future process participants or other stakeholders.

Weekly meeting

Two employees are designing a new structure for their department's weekly meetings. The weekly meeting is an organizational classic. Weekly meetings come in many different forms, but they all have something in common: they are repeated every week, and the participants know both the routine and the culture.

Here is an example of how two co-workers can use the Process Designer to design a new process for their department's weekly meeting.

The background for the weekly meeting is that the department needs a fixed routine that ensures that employees share knowledge with one another. *The purpose* is to share knowledge and jointly handle the most important tasks of the week. *The goal* of the weekly meeting is for everyone to become informed of one another's work and the most important tasks of the week. *The result* is a prioritized list of tasks that must be solved by specific persons within a given timeframe. *The participants* are the department's staff and the meeting is led by the department manager. *The prin-*

ciples that must ensure that the goals and results of the weekly meeting are achieved are that everyone listens to learn, shares the most important information, and thinks in a problem-solving way. *The situation*: A one-hour meeting every Monday in meeting room 202, with a projector and whiteboard available. *The process steps* include:

– Welcome from the manager
– Brief reports from all employees
– Open dialogue about reports
– Summary: Roles and division of responsibility for the week.

Participant experience: Before the meeting, the participants wish to talk about their work tasks, and they are eager to hear about what tasks their colleagues have. After the meeting the participants will have gained a better understanding of one another's work, and they feel ready to tackle their work for the week. *Next steps*: After the meeting the meeting manager sends out a summary email with prioritized tasks and deadlines to all meeting participants, and the tasks are completed.

Two employees are designing a new structure for their department's weekly meetings.

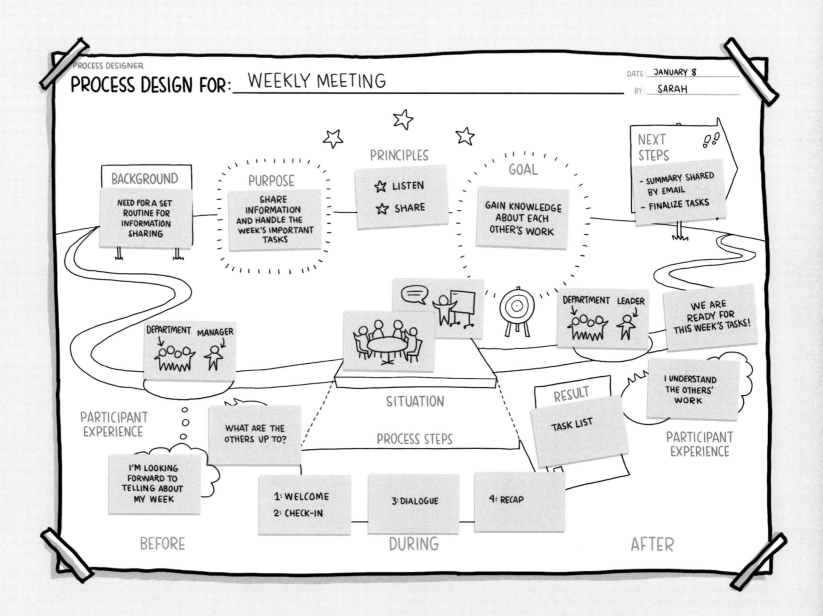

Strategy workshop

A workshop is a working method where a group is assembled to work in a concentrated and practical way to solve a specific task.

Here is an example of how the executive board of an organization can use the Process Designer to design a strategy workshop for their senior management team.

The background for holding the workshop is the executive board's wish to present a new strategy they have developed for upper management's approval. *The purpose* of the workshop is to introduce and fine-tune the new strategy together with the management group. *The goal* is for the management group to take ownership of the new strategy. *The result* is a completed template with answers to the four strategic questions. *The participants* are the ten most senior managers, two members from the executive board, and a facilitator. *The principles* guiding the work include dialogue, relevance, and participation.

The situation is a two-hour session with whiteboard, template, and drawing/writing materials.

The process steps consist of:

– welcome and introduction
– strategy presentation
– dialogue on the four strategic questions
– summary and next steps.

Participant experience: Before the workshop the managers will be curious about the new strategy. During the workshop, most will be overwhelmingly positive, but aspects of the strategy may stir doubts in some. After the workshop, everyone will feel that they have been heard, and that they have had their part in shaping the content of the strategy.
Next steps: After the workshop, input from managers shall be implemented, and the strategy shall be rolled out to the rest of the organization.

An executive board plans a strategy workshop for their organization's 10 most senior managers.

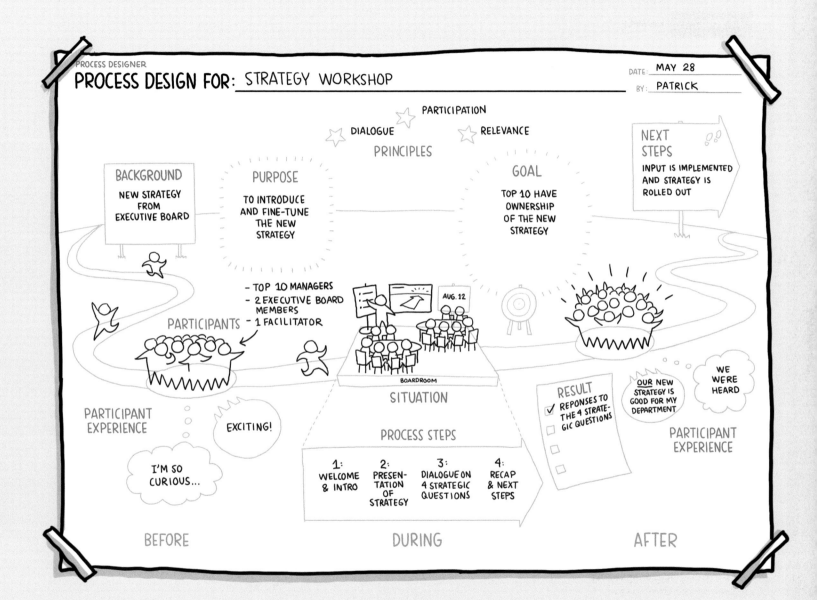

Summary

Good preparation: Ten process questions can help you and your team design almost any process.

Process Designer: If you work visually with your process questions in the Process Designer, you will create an overview and ensure cohesion in your process design.

Application: The tool can be used alone or in groups to brainstorm, select, group, and formulate the most important elements of a process.

Examples: The Process Designer and the ten process questions can be used for all types of processes where people interact. You can add your own additional questions or elements to fit your next process.

FOR WHICH PROCESS
WOULD IT BE VALUABLE
FOR YOU TO CREATE A
PROCESS DESIGN?

Aligned by shared purpose

2014 Sorø Meeting: A visual, jointly created vision for the youth education programs of tomorrow

Purpose: To explore how we jointly create tomorrow's youth education programs that all youth complete and that produce people capable of meeting life's challenges

Principles:
– Active participation
– Visualization
– Co-creation
– Relevance
– Forward-looking perspective 2020+

Goal: To inspire one another and create milestones for tomorrow's youth education program

Contents: Introduction, group work, presentations, plenary discussions, etc.

Results:
– A common picture of the vision for tomorrow's youth education programs
– Inspiration and guidelines for tomorrow's youth education programs
– Personal immediate next steps for participants on sticky notes
– Each participant has 3 new telephone numbers

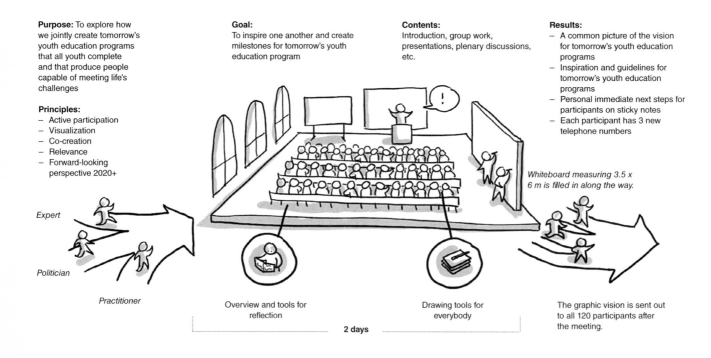

Expert

Politician

Practitioner

Overview and tools for reflection

Drawing tools for everybody

Whiteboard measuring 3.5 x 6 m is filled in along the way.

The graphic vision is sent out to all 120 participants after the meeting.

2 days

The Sorø Meeting: In the early 1980s, then Minister of Education Bertel Haarder started the tradition of inviting school teachers, experts, practitioners, artists, and politicians to Sorø Academy in Copenhagen, Denmark, to debate current topics in educational policy.

In 2014 the meeting addressed future educational programs for young people, and it was here that then Minister of Education Christine Antorini chose to employ visual facilitation as a working method before, during, and after the meeting.

Given the minister's tightly packed schedule, it was impossible for her to participate in all of the deliberations and decisions that were to be made in conjunction with a meeting like Sorø.

By working visually in the early planning phase, the process, content, and results of the meeting were solidified through visualizations.

Many organizations or networks hold meetings or conferences to share knowledge and "think together," and here the Sorø Meeting was no exception. A key detail in this case, however, is the fact that participants are invited because they are politically engaged in the subject of the meeting. They are therefore not part of the same organization and are not necessarily working toward the same vision or don't hold the same perspective on how it should be achieved.

The participants at the Sorø Meeting are in this sense a diverse group, and mapping the different participants was therefore a determining factor in terms of successfully being able to jointly create a vision for tomorrow's youth education programs that the participants could own, if not as a whole then at least in the parts that they personally had helped formulate and visualize.

The results of the meeting, a visual vision for the youth education programs of the future, were subsequently sent out to all 120 participants so they could share their experiences from the meeting and continue dialoguing on tomorrow's educational programs back in their own organizations or networks.

"As a minister you make a lot of decisions. It is therefore paramount to have a network of skilled partners you can rely on to clarify a subject, take ownership, and make decisions on an informed basis. The visual work approach that the project group used in planning the 2014 Sorø Meeting made it easy for us to see how the meeting unfolded, where we could make adjustments to make sure we had a process where everyone could really have influence."

Christine Antorini
Danish Minister of Education, 2011–2015

3.
Define key questions

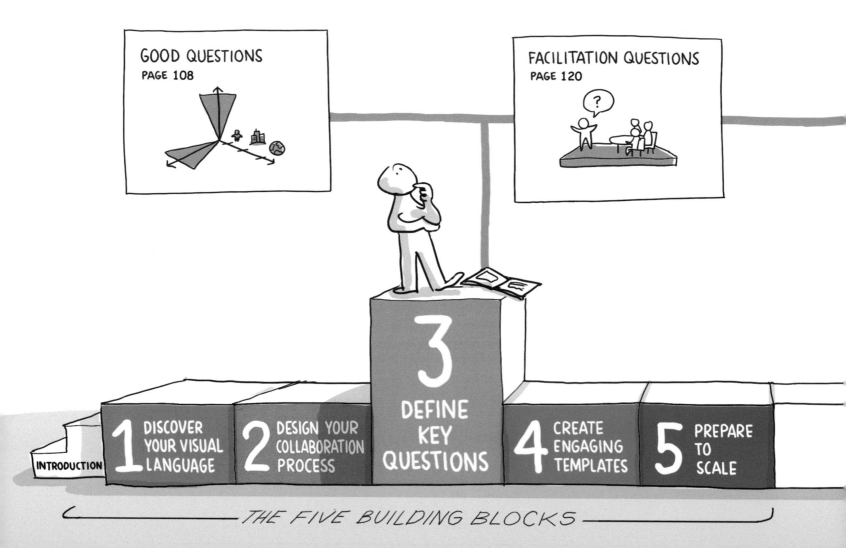

GOAL: YOU HAVE A SET OF IMPACTFUL QUESTIONS FOR YOUR NEXT MEETING, PROJECT, OR PROCESS

VISUALIZATION QUESTIONS
PAGE 126

TOOL: QUESTION DESIGNER
PAGE 136

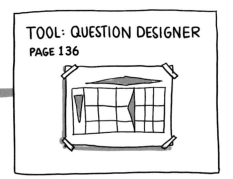

6 ENABLE GROUP LEARNING

7 MAP YOUR SKILLS

8 ACTIVATE YOUR RESOURCES

9 DO'S & DON'TS

Good questions

Our lives are given fundamental meaning by the questions we ask and that are asked of us.

People's ability to reflect on the world and ask questions has been essential to progress and development. "What does it mean to be human?" This was the question posed by Søren Kierkegaard. The search for answers consumed the whole of his brief life and laid the foundation of existentialism. "How can we create a free, living, natural people's enlightenment?" asked N.F.S. Grundtvig, laying the foundation of the Danish public school system.

What will I be when I grow up? What matters most to me? What should I study? Where will I live? With whom? Questions set a direction and focus our attention. Whether we are dealing with fundamental, personal, or organizational questions, good questions inspire us to seek meaningful answers. It is therefore worth spending the time to formulate good questions.

"If I had an hour to solve a problem I'd spend 55 minutes thinking about the problem and 5 minutes thinking about solutions. Because when I know the question, I can solve the problem in less than five minutes."

—Attributed to Albert Einstein

We gather around questions. Many organizations, projects, and meetings have been created to find answers to one or more shared important questions.

"How can we create a better everyday life for the many people?"

If you work at IKEA, this is a well-known question examined on a daily basis across departments and hierarchies, even today, more than 70 years after IKEA was founded (Ingvar Kamprad, "Testament of a Furniture Dealer," 1976).

"How can we create educational programs, which everyone can complete, and that foster young people capable of meeting life's challenges?"

Then Minister of Education Christine Antorini asked the above question at the 2014 annual summit in Sorø. She brought together 120 experts on education for two days of dialogue on the development of Danish youth education.

"How can we accelerate the use of pen and paper and show the world that it is at least as important to learn to draw as it is to learn to read, write, and count?"

This is the question driving us in our work at Bigger Picture.

Good facilitation questions support your process design. In the previous chapter we introduced ten questions that could help you create a cohesive process design. In this chapter we show how questions can support your process design: How can you design questions that fit the purpose of your process, help the process forward toward its goal, and ensure that concrete results are created that can be used in the future?

What questions are most relevant for the participants in your next process?

The path to dialogue

When a good question is addressed to a group, it works like an invitation to examine, discover, and explore great answers together.

A good facilitator promotes and stimulates constructive dialogue by offering a focused framework, asking guiding questions, and suggesting adjustments as necessary. The goal is for a group to get to the point where they "think" together, creating new and productive ideas together and developing and sharing new insights. The path to dialogue requires that the group members can speak and listen openly and honestly to one another without resistance. As a facilitator, you can support this by using various types of questions combined in a particular sequence:

– *In the beginning* of a process, it is useful to ask questions that explicitly refer to the talk-in-turns principle and create an expectation that participants listen to one another.
– *The middle of a process* benefits from exploratory and open-ended questions.
– *The end* of the process calls for more reflective and closing questions.

Our path to good dialogues was inspired by the American management coach William Isaacs and is presented in simplified form here. The definitions of dialogue and discussion are ours, as are the various examples of questions.

On Isaacs's path to good dialogue we face a choice in every conversation: We can choose to suspend judgment and remain open, or we can choose to judge another person's position and defend our own. Advocates who defend their own position are cut off from one another, and as a result, each ends up thinking on their own. If, instead, participants choose to suspend judgment, dialogue brings them closer together, and then it becomes possible to think together. As a facilitator your challenge is to design questions, and facilitate the conversation about them, in a way that helps groups think together. The goal is a reflective learning dialogue in which participants jointly develop shared meanings and insights rather than simply exchanging opinions.

DIALOGUE

Origin: from Greek *dialogos*, "conversation."
Our definition: A dialogue is a collective process where those involved jointly examine, explore, and discover— through speech, text, or drawing—new perspectives on a given subject.

DISCUSSION

Origin: from Latin *discutere*, "to break into pieces."
Our definition: A discussion is a crossroads where opposing views meet (in speech, text, or drawing), where positions are marked, and where individuals define their boundaries.

The talk-in-turns principle:
– Emma, what do you expect from this collaboration?

Shows active listening:
– Robert, what is the most important thing you heard Jane say?
– Where do you see similarities between the perspectives we have heard?

Supports reflective dialogue:
– When you say X, Sofia, what is this based on?
– Why is it important to focus on X?

Supports learning dialogue:
– On the basis of what we have heard, what is the best way forward?

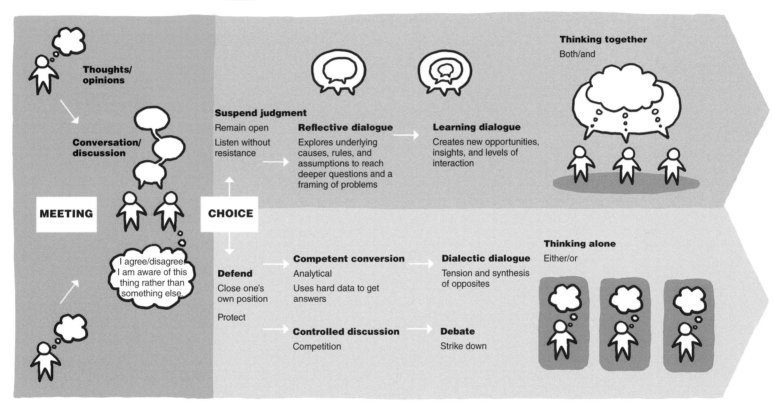

Function of the question

As a facilitator, questions are your most important tool. They develop, engage, inspire innovation, and enable good dialogues.

Opening and closing dialogues. The function and timing of the question are important to consider when designing a series of questions for a process. Some questions are open-ended and invite numerous and diverse answers. Others are closed and call for conclusion, choices, and decisions. Working with the function of a question and placing it where it best fits in the process is important for the flow of the process, the participants' experience, and the content of the answers that participants can produce.

When we design a series of questions for a process, we therefore do it with what we call the process diamond in the back of our minds. The process diamond is an interpretation of Sam Kaner's "Diamond of Participatory Decision-Making," which he presents in his book *The Facilitator's Guide to Participatory Decision-Making*. We have simplified Kaner's diamond slightly to focus here on the various functions that facilitation questions have and on their placement in the process.

According to Kaner, a facilitation process can be divided into three zones: the *divergent zone*, the *"groan zone,"* and the *convergent zone*.

The process diamond

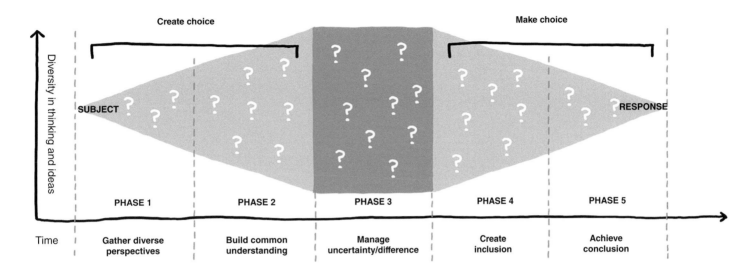

FUNCTION OF THE QUESTION

Create choice

Make choice

Diversity in thinking and ideas

SUBJECT

RESPONSE

PHASE 1 | PHASE 2 | PHASE 3 | PHASE 4 | PHASE 5

Time

Gather diverse perspectives | Build common understanding | Manage uncertainty/difference | Create inclusion | Achieve conclusion

THE DIVERGENT ZONE:
PHASES 1 AND 2

In the divergent, opening zone, there is freedom and openness. Different perspectives are collected here, and alternatives are sought. This is an open phase where participants are trained to say "yes/and" rather than "no/but." This zone is fundamentally about creating shared knowledge on a given subject or question. In this opening zone there is space for a high degree of diversity in thinking and ideas. There are two phases in the divergent zone. Phase 1 asks questions that invite open and diverse answers. Questions in Phase 2 promote the formation of a broad common framework of understanding.

GROAN ZONE:
PHASE 3

The groan zone is a point in a process where confusion and frustration usually arise in participants. Here, the complexity of the subject or question is most obvious, and participants may feel there is no clear way forward from this point. In this Phase 3 zone, the function of the question is to help the group manage and accept difference and uncertainty. The questions must be designed so they support the participants in tackling frustration and finding a way forward.

THE CONVERGENT ZONE:
PHASES 4 AND 5

In the convergent, closing zone, participants shall evaluate what they have created. They must summarize key points, prioritize, and group their knowledge for final conclusion. The group must collectively take responsibility for what they have produced. The convergent zone comprises the end phases of the process, Phases 4 and 5. The function of the questions in Phase 4 is to get participants to create cohesion by connecting and grouping their content. In Phase 5 the questions must be formulated so they clearly call on participants to make decisions and conclude the process.

The process diamond at the macro and micro levels

The role and responsibility of a facilitator is to design and facilitate a series of steps where participants jointly find answers to a subject or question. By working with questions and their various functions in the three zones of the process diamond, the facilitator helps the process and its participants move forward.

The process diamond can be used at both the macro and micro levels. At the macro level you can design an entire process, with related series of questions, according to the three zones of the diamond. At the micro level you can use the process diamond to design a series of help questions that dive down into one of the overarching questions of the process. At both levels, the series of questions are designed on the basis of the three zones of the diamond.

On page 94 in the previous building block, the process diamond is seen used at the micro level for the question "What is the purpose of the process?"

MACRO LEVEL

Questions are entered into the process diamond so that they jointly provide an answer to the overall question: What is our 2030 strategy?

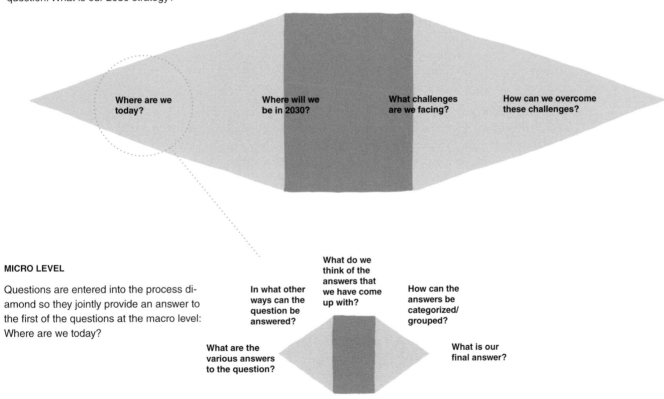

Where are we today?

Where will we be in 2030?

What challenges are we facing?

How can we overcome these challenges?

MICRO LEVEL

Questions are entered into the process diamond so they jointly provide an answer to the first of the questions at the macro level: Where are we today?

What do we think of the answers that we have come up with?

In what other ways can the question be answered?

How can the answers be categorized/grouped?

What are the various answers to the question?

What is our final answer?

Question architecture

Design your questions based on three dimensions: the question's structure, its assumption, and its scope—this gives you a good starting point to create good questions that promote insight, innovation, and action.

THREE DIMENSIONS

"The usefulness of the knowledge we acquire and the effectiveness of the actions we take depend on the quality of the questions we ask," wrote Eric E. Vogt, Juanita Brown, and David Isaacs in their article "The Art of Powerful Questions." In this article they also present the three-dimensional rule for what they call "the architecture of good questions."

They identify the three dimensions of effective questions for building a framework for a learning dialogue and opening the door to discovery. The three dimensions are structure, assumption, and scope.

Questions designed with all three dimensions in mind promote insight, innovation, and action.

In this section you can see how we work with the three dimensions.

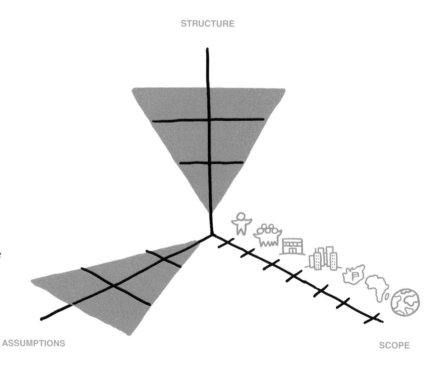

STRUCTURE

ASSUMPTIONS

SCOPE

116

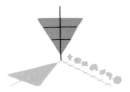

STRUCTURE

Some questions open the way to many answers. They take a wide-angle view of what they are asking about. Others are more closed and narrow in their structure, and may only allow the possibility of a yes or no answer, for example.

When working with the structure of a question, you can use the question triangle to examine the robustness of the question.

Here is an example of how a question changes from the bottom of the triangle to the top:

– At bottom: *Are you satisfied with our collaboration?*
– In the middle: *When have you been most satisfied with our collaboration?*
– At top: *What in our collaboration do you find most satisfactory?*
– Topmost: *Why do you think that our collaboration has its ups and downs?*

The higher up in the triangle the question rises, the more it invites reflection and dialogue. A question at the top of the triangle is not necessarily more important or better than the questions at the bottom of the triangle. The questions you ask depend on the purpose of the situation or process in which the question is to be asked.

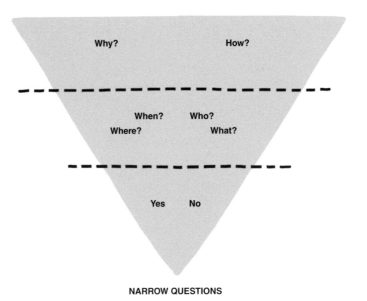

BROAD QUESTIONS

Why?　　　　How?

When?　Who?
Where?　　What?

Yes　No

NARROW QUESTIONS

SCOPE

The scope of your question is significant to your recipient. If a question is too broad, it can drain energy from the person being asked and have a demotivating effect. To encourage engagement, questions need to be relevant and realistic for us to answer. *"How can we make the world a better place?"* is a very broad and sometimes overwhelming question, whereas *"How can we reduce our department's CO_2 footprint?"* is a question that is more manageable and easier to act on.

A question can, however, also be too narrow and limited for your recipient's way of thinking: *"How can we improve our mutual communication?"* focuses only on the communication rather than this slightly broader question: *"How can we improve collaboration in our team?"*

A question must be tailored to its purpose, and it must be neither so broad that the recipient becomes paralyzed nor so narrow that the answers become navel-gazing.

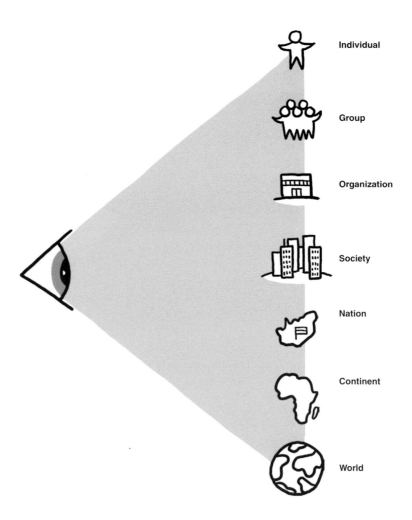

Individual

Group

Organization

Society

Nation

Continent

World

ASSUMPTIONS

Questions often contain hidden assumptions. These are frequently embedded in the language and are difficult to avoid. It is important that we are aware of the assumptions on which our questions are based and work with them strategically.

How can we create better cross-collaboration?

This question assumes that the recipients agree cross-collaboration needs to be improved. Wishing to avoid this implicit negativity, one might instead ask:

What characterizes our working methods when we are at our best in terms of cross-collaboration?

The implicit assumption is positive: that the recipient has good experiences with respect to cross-collaboration. This validation creates more motivation in the response process.

It can be useful to bring a group's assumptions (as evidenced in statements or questions) out into the light by explicitly asking them:

What are the assumptions we are basing this conversation on?

How might we approach this if we saw it from the perspective of our co-workers?

Examining underlying assumptions can support the generation of new perspectives.

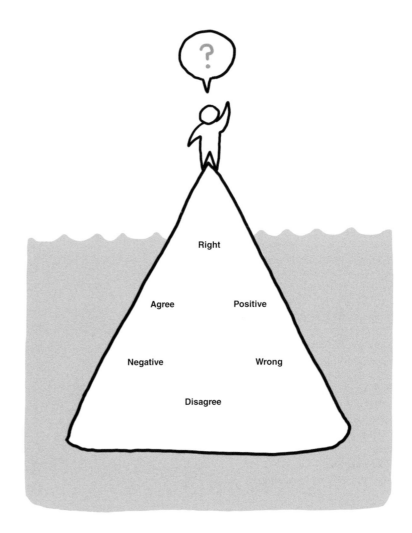

Facilitation questions

Divide your facilitation questions into three categories: subject-oriented questions, results-oriented questions, and process-oriented questions—and use them actively to guide your participants.

THREE CATEGORIES

A large part of a facilitator's skill resides in the ability to ask good questions. Good questions are also well timed and diverse. Effective process design and good questions promote participation, build common understanding, support inclusive solutions, and cultivate common responsibility for the goals and results of the process. In addition to questions that focus on the subject at hand, it is important to prepare questions that promote group collaboration and allow for the evaluation of results. These help the group view results along the way, and observe and validate collaboration and common learning.

We divide our facilitation questions into three categories.

SUBJECT-ORIENTED QUESTIONS:

Questions relating directly to what the participants are meeting about—the topic and purpose of the process.

RESULTS-ORIENTED QUESTIONS:

Questions that get participants to review and consider the results they are creating or have already created.

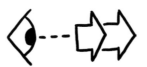

PROCESS-ORIENTED QUESTIONS

Questions that get participants to review and consider the way they are working together in the process.

Subject-oriented questions

The purpose of the process and your process design determine what subject-oriented questions should be asked. These questions have the subject at their core. The sum of the subject-oriented questions should, by the conclusion of the process, provide the desired answers and the results that were formulated in the process design.

To the right are some examples of subject-oriented questions for two different subjects and their related processes. The questions were designed on the basis of the two process designs we reviewed at the end of the previous building block. Some subject-oriented questions will be obvious. At other times they require a little more time and consideration. Once you have arrived at your series of questions, work with each question individually and refine its architecture. Even if a question appears immediately obvious, it may upon closer review prove to include assumptions that are not suitable for your purposes.

Also look at your series of questions as a whole and prioritize the questions in relation to how well they fulfill their function in the process. Vary your way of asking the questions so your participants are engaged and inspired to have new ideas or approach the subject from new angles.

EXAMPLE

A group of managers are developing their strategy with you as facilitator.

Examples of subject-oriented questions for various processes

SUBJECT/PROCESS	WEEKLY MEETING	STRATEGY WORKSHOP
Purpose	To share knowledge and handle the important tasks of the week	To introduce and fine-tune the new strategy
Goal	Learning about one another's work	Senior manager takes ownership of the new strategy
Results	Task list	Answers to four strategic questions
Subject-oriented questions	– What are the most important tasks we have each worked on independently since the last weekly meeting? – What is the most important thing each of us learned since the last weekly meeting? – What is the most important thing that must happen or be done by each of us over the next week? – What can we learn on the basis of the knowledge that we have shared today? – What questions does this prompt? – What question is it most import-ant to find an answer to? – Who does what and when until the next weekly meeting?	– Why do we exist? – Why do we have to change? – What would happen if we did nothing? – What characterizes where we are today? – Who are we? – What are our weaknesses? – What are our strengths? – What characterizes where we would like to be in 2030? – What does it look like when we succeed? – What challenges do we need to overcome to succeed? – What initiatives can tackle our challenges?

SEE ALSO
Subject-oriented questions from three known templates:

SWOT
– What are our strengths?
– What are our weaknesses?
– What opportunities do we see?
– What threats do we see?

Project planning (Game Plan)
– Who is in the project group?
– What tasks do we need to get underway?
– What phases do we have?
– What are our goals?
– What drivers help the process along the way?
– What challenges might arise along the way?

Business model generation
– What are our core values?
– What are our core activities?
– What are our core resources?
– What are our customer relationships?
– What channels do we have to reach customers?
– What are our customer segments?
– Who are our partners?
– What are our costs?
– What are our revenues?

Results-oriented questions

Results-oriented questions can be used along the way in a process where parts of the results are created, and at the conclusion of the process, when the results are available in their final form.

The purpose of results-oriented questions is, among other things, to promote full and active participation by observing the group's performance along the way. The questions can encourage the group to deliver more or do it better. When a group jointly observes what it is in the process of creating, or has created, the process builds shared ownership and refreshes responsibility for the goals and results of the process. Results-oriented questions can also encourage more inclusive solutions. By observing results from different perspectives people become aware of new connections or challenges. With the right timing, results-oriented questions can lead to valuable mid-course corrections that improve the process and its results.

Results-oriented questions also help participants be specific in their answers, because they specifically reference what the group has just created.

Examples of results-oriented questions

- What is the most important conclusion we have reached so far?
- What can support or challenge what we have determined?
- What characterizes the progress we have made?
- What might others say about the progress we have made?
- Who will derive benefit from the results?
- When might what we have concluded no longer be relevant?
- Where can we seek inspiration to make the results even better?
- What questions may others ask that could challenge our decisions or create new or different answers?
- What makes the results to date good or useful?
- Are there other considerations to take into account when looking at our results?

Process-oriented questions

Asking process-oriented questions is a good way to work with group dynamics.

When we use process-oriented questions, it's like holding a mirror up to the group participants and asking them what they see. They are a tool for self-observation and can advance self-regulation if any dysfunction has developed. They can also help participants notice what is working well. And they can get a group to adjust a schedule if this proves necessary to achieve the right solution.

Process-oriented questions are also essential to organizational learning. When we answer these questions, we evaluate the way in which we work together. The answers can therefore serve to guide us when we design the next process. If you are conducting a long-term project in a team, process-oriented questions ensure that you both reach targets in your project and also accumulate learning and develop better working methods along the way.

Examples of process-oriented questions

- What have you noticed so far?
- Why is this process important for us?
- How are you feeling about this process?
- How can we best move forward from here?
- What can we improve going forward?
- Who else would like to be included in this process?
- When would it be appropriate to take a break?
- Where in the process did the group have the most or least energy?
- What three things could we do to challenge ourselves in this process?

EXAMPLE

A group of managers are developing their strategy with you as facilitator.

Visualization questions

Divide your visualization questions into three categories: image creation questions, image relation questions, and image application questions—and use them to create and develop your visual learning arena.

THREE CATEGORIES

When you work visually, you also need an additional set of questions—your visualization questions. These are questions that can help your participants to *"see what they each think."* But they are also questions that help solidify the visual dimension and help you and your participants create, develop, and utilize your visual learning arena.

Visualization questions are important when you work visually. Like other questions, they require attention and timing. A visualization question can be associated with a conventional facilitation question and bring new life to it. On its own it can also invite a group to see new connections and discover new opportunities. But if the timing is not right, or if the formulation is off, a visualization question can also short-circuit a process. It can lock a group into a particular way of thinking or a specific visual language, or it may be too specific at a time when this is not appropriate.

We work with three categories of visualization questions: image creation questions, image relation questions, and image application questions. As a whole, all visualization questions help you and your participants to build your own visual language, adapted to the matters you work with. The visualization questions also ensure that you have pressure-tested your visualizations along the way.

IMAGE CREATION QUESTIONS

Questions that stimulate the participants' imagination by asking for mental or physical visualizations.

IMAGE RELATION QUESTIONS

Questions that get participants to review and consider a visualization.

IMAGE APPLICATION QUESTIONS

Questions that get participants to reflect on working visually.

Image creation questions

When a facilitator asks his or her participants: *"What characterizes where we are today?"* and then further asks: *"… and what does it look like? How might we draw it?"* images are created by the group.

"What does it look like?" is the visual facilitator's most important image creation question. This question stimulates the imagination of participants, and it helps them to become concrete in their answers. "What does it look like?" is therefore a good question to ask in many variations. See the examples to the right, and come up with more of your own.

Image creating questions are often the questions that give your participants a sense of co-creation and ownership. Perhaps not every participant has a marker in hand along the way, but they have been involved in devising, formulating, and creating the visual language that at the end of the process forms their overall picture. They know the logic behind each visualization. Even if they did not invent it on their own, they heard it explained by the creator(s) and approved it as part of the development process. This creates shared ownership with respect to the final products of the process.

EXAMPLE

A group of managers are developing their strategy with you as facilitator.

Examples

Your image creation questions also give you the opportunity to map out a topic in space. Relational terms help us describe relationships between places, things, people, and points in time. Image creation questions that promote relational descriptions are important when you wish to draw and manage the complexity that is often inherent in our organizations and projects. To the right are a few examples of questions that promote relationship descriptions in the image creation process.

You can also ensure good variation in your "What does it look like" questions by focusing on these elements in your visual language:
- things: the artifacts of the subject
- people: those involved and their characteristics, feelings, relationships, roles, responsibilities, and tasks
- time and place: where and when something happens
- process: how it happens.

Variations: What does it look like?	Variations: Questions that advance visual language	Variations: Questions that advance relationship description
– How can it be drawn? – How can it be visualized? – If we had to draw what you are saying, what would it look like? – What images does it generate? – What associations does it create? – If we took a photo of it, what would be in the picture?	– How would you describe a situation or event where what you recounted took place? – What metaphors would be used to describe it? – What narrative would give a good picture of what you are describing?	– What relationship/placement do the elements you are describing have toward one another? (For example, quantity, distance, size, hierarchy, sequence, priority) – How can what you are describing be laid out visually? – What is the form/color/structure of what you are describing?

Things	People	Time/Place	Processes
– What relevant tools can we visualize; what do they look like? – What artifact could be a good metaphor for what you are describing? – What physical tools or things should we include to create recognition?	– Who is involved and what do they look like (team, management, users, etc.)? – How can we visually show the different roles they have?	– Where is it happening, and how does it look? – When is it happening, and how does it look? – What characterizes the situation right now, and what does it look like?	– What does the process look like before, during, and after? – What do steps three to five of the process look like? – What does it look like when we succeed? – What is the essence of what you are doing in your organization/team/department, and what does it look like?

Image relation questions

Image relation questions are only relevant once you have created visual material, either on your own or as a group. They help you to fine-tune and develop the visual material that you have created. In answering these questions you will often find yourself and your participants moving. Your visualizations have become the focus of the dialogue, and you are actively working with what you have created. Your conversations, presentations, and discussions are literally written on the walls. You can therefore focus the dialogue and refer back by pointing to what has already been created.

The physical objects and your image relation questions make it easier for your participants to move between different levels of observation and serve to get participants to take a position toward the visual. The participants thereby become co-creators and co-owners of what is on the walls. The greater their involvement in the development of visual material, the more they will own and use it afterwards.

Image relation questions sometimes seem to be of limited use in the moment. But when an image is out of balance, or an employee group can't come up with a visualization of a structural change in the organization, it can have major consequences.

Examples of image relation questions

- How do you see what we have drawn?
- What does the drawing show?
- What does the drawing not show?
- What insights does this picture provide?
- What questions does this picture raise?
- What can improve the drawing?
- How else could the picture be interpreted?
- What works well/less well in the drawing?
- What is clear/unclear in this picture?
- What should there be more/less of?
- What could be omitted/added?
- If X was not included, what would happen?
- If others were to look at this, what would they say about it?
- What is most important in the drawing?
- What elements belong together?
- What elements do not belong in this drawing?
- What patterns/themes do we see?
- What relationships are apparent in the drawing?
- What basic assumptions are implicit in this picture?
- How could we work with the colors so as to highlight the relationships that you mention?

A group of managers is developing their strategy
with you as visual facilitator.

Image application questions

The third category is about getting your participants to reflect about working visually. It helps ensure that what you have just created is relevant and used appropriately.

An image application question can also be used to shake things up a little. If you ask *"What drawing would be good to get everyone in the organization talking about?"* you are asking your participants to think in images BEFORE linguistic formulation. This is an exercise that can launch new perspectives and understanding.

Image application questions, like the process-oriented questions, are a tool for gauging the perceived value in a visual way of working. The answers can inform how you use visual approaches in the next processes and projects you facilitate. Image application questions offer participants the opportunity to evaluate strengths and weaknesses in the visual work approach. It ensures that going forward you work visually in the projects and processes where it adds value... – and try a different approach where it does not.

Examples of image application questions

– What resulted from having a drawing about what we were talking about?
– How did it work to produce a drawing as a team?
– What effect did the drawing have in our dialogue about X?
– When does it work and when does it not work to draw?
– How can drawings promote/inhibit the overall process?
– What power is there in wielding the pen?
– What was it like to draw?
– What characterizes your/our drawing style?
– What characterizes what we have drawn?
– What was it like to use a drawing as a basis for conversation?
– What was it like to see other people's drawings?
– What was difficult/easy about drawing X?
– What would it take for us to want to draw more?
– What drawing could be used to catalyze an important dialogue in our organization?
– How would you like to use the drawings we have created?

EXAMPLE

A group of managers is developing their strategy
with you as visual facilitator.

Question test

Test the questions you've formulated. If you can reply
yes to half of the criteria questions below, that's a good
indicator that your question works. Remember that it is
always the purpose of your process that should guide you.

Is the question…

1. RELEVANT

Is the question relevant for the
people concerned? Is it relevant with respect to their lives
and work? Is it relevant for the
agreed purpose?

2. UNANSWERED

Is the question authentic,
one to which the answer is
unknown, and one that is
worthwhile for others to meet
about?

3. INNOVATIVE

Does the question incite new
ideas and creativity? Is the
question both recognizable
and relevant for the recipient
and yet enough of a departure
to produce new answers?

4. APPRECIATIVE

Does the question generate
a sense of hope and engagement? Is it positive and
forward-looking, or does it
focus on the problems and
obstacles of the past?

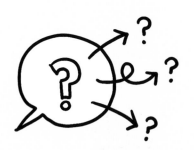   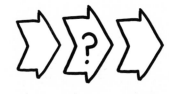

5. INSPIRING

Does the question spark new and different questions that produce new perspectives?

6. EASY TO REMEMBER

Is the question hard to let go once you have heard it? Does it draw people in to try to find better answers?

7. VISUAL

Does the question stimulate your recipient's imagination? Is it specific or metaphorical, or does it otherwise help support the creation of a visual language that promotes understanding and resonance?

8. TIMELY

Is the question in the right sequence with respect to the function it has in the process?

TOOL

Question Designer

Good questions are long-lived. Use this tool to design the questions you will work with in your next process.

HOW?
Work with the Question Designer as shown on the next page. After the five steps, select the questions you will use in your next process.

STICKY NOTES
Use sticky notes so you can move around and try different questions.

HOW COULD
YOU ALSO
DRAW IT?

 Download the Question Designer on www.visualcollaboration.site.

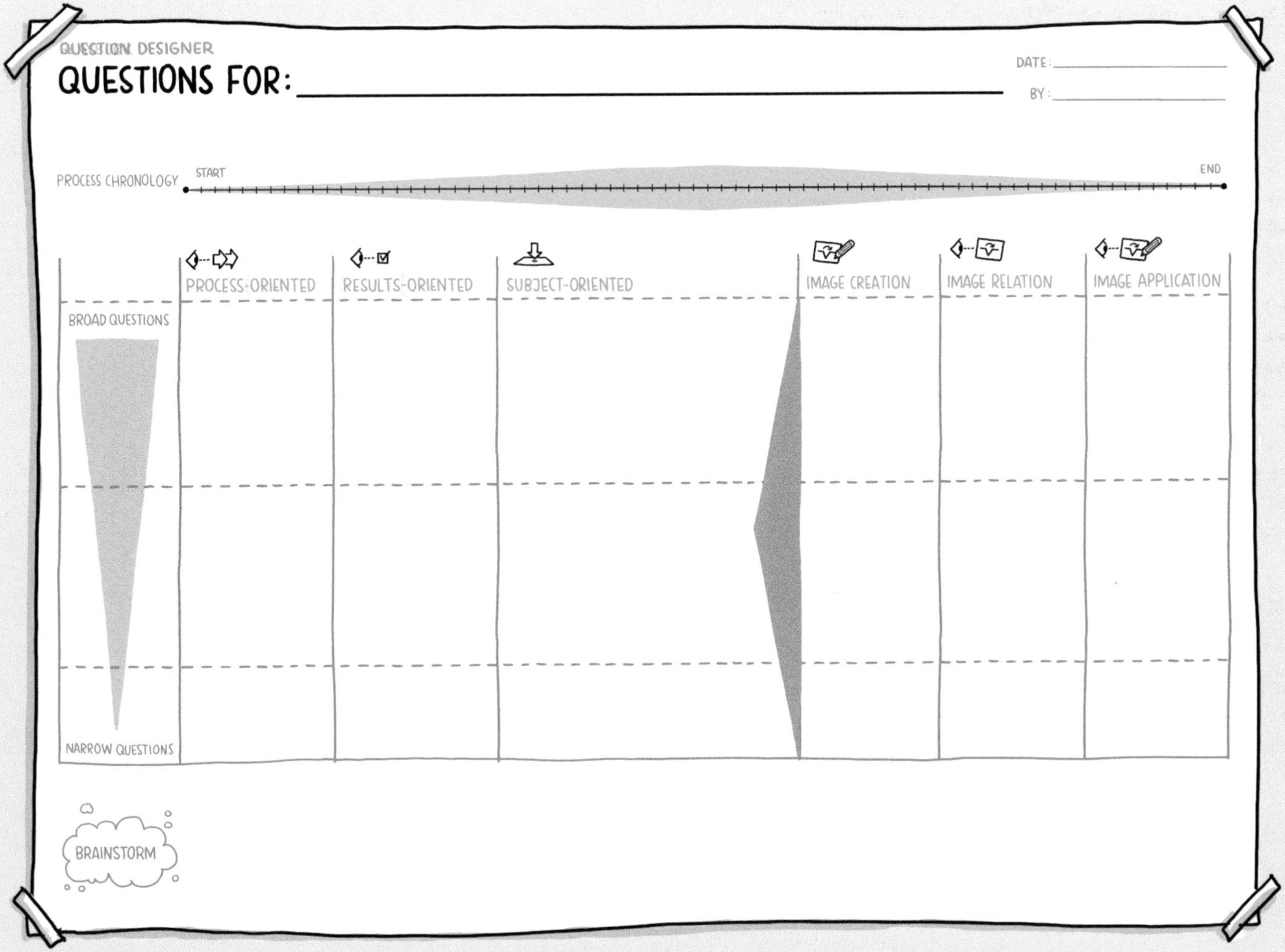

QUESTION DESIGNER

QUESTIONS FOR: _____

DATE: _____

BY: _____

PROCESS CHRONOLOGY   START |—————————————————————————————| END

	PROCESS-ORIENTED	RESULTS-ORIENTED	SUBJECT-ORIENTED	IMAGE CREATION	IMAGE RELATION	IMAGE APPLICATION
BROAD QUESTIONS						
NARROW QUESTIONS						

BRAINSTORM

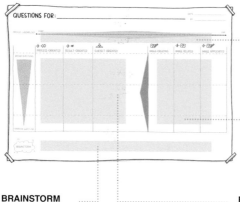

BRAINSTORM

List questions that might be relevant for your process design.

Use sticky notes to brainstorm on all the questions that may be relevant for your process design. Write one question per sticky note. Review your process design and consider what questions can be asked in each part of the process. Place the questions in the field arbitrarily. Formulate as many questions as possible, and preferably include a few wild, outside-the-box questions. Wait to screen out the ones that aren't as strong.

FACILITATION QUESTIONS

Place your questions in the three categories of facilitation questions.

Take sticky notes from your brainstorming field and place them in whichever of the three categories that fits best.
- Subject-oriented: Questions that relate directly to what the participants are meeting about.
- Results-oriented: Questions that get the participants to think about the results they are creating or have created.
- Process-oriented: Questions that get participants to think about the way they gather and exchange ideas.

Shift the sticky notes around so they reflect the structure of the questions. "Why" questions at the top and "Yes/no" questions at the bottom. Select the best and most important. Reformulate questions so they change position in the triangle, or so completely new ones arise. Let the ones that are not as good stay in the Brainstorm field. Make sure that you have at least three good questions in each category.

VISUALIZATION QUESTIONS

List questions that can help create visual material.
- Image creation: Questions that stimulate the participants' imaginations.
- Image relation: Questions that get participants to review and consider a visualization.
- Image application: Questions that get participants to think about what happens when we work visually.

Use small symbols to show where you will work with image creation questions. Example: The question *"What does it look like?"* has a star symbol. Draw stars on the facilitation questions where you also wish to use the follow-up question *"What does it look like?"*

CHRONOLOGY

Arrange your questions in a series along the three zones of the process diamond.
- Open and exploratory questions for the divergent zone
- Confidence-inspiring and process-advancing questions go to the groan zone
- Closing and concluding questions for the converging zone

TEST

Review each of your questions, and test them by considering:
- What assumptions are hidden here?
- Does this question fit the purpose of the process?
- Can the question be formulated in other ways that work better?
- Does the question have the right reach?
- Review the eight questions from the question test on page 134 and revise if necessary.

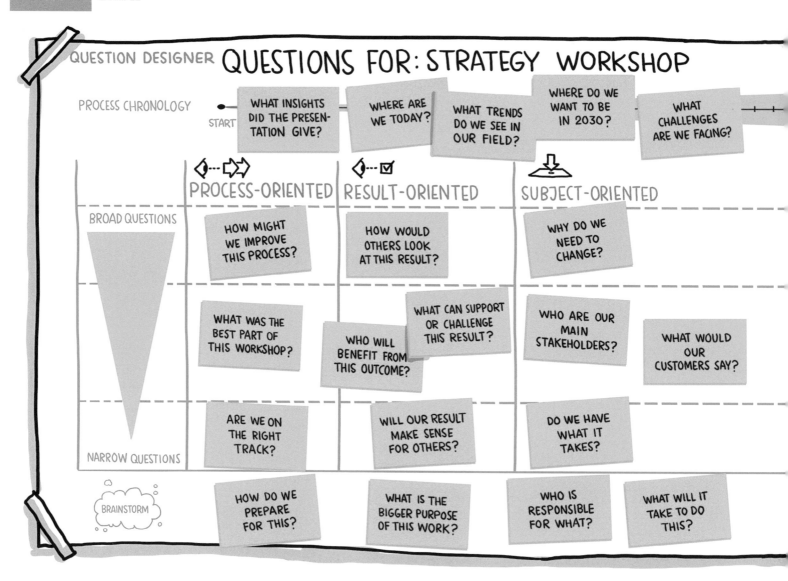

QUESTION DESIGNER

QUESTIONS FOR: STRATEGY WORKSHOP

PROCESS CHRONOLOGY

START

- WHAT INSIGHTS DID THE PRESENTATION GIVE?
- WHERE ARE WE TODAY?
- WHAT TRENDS DO WE SEE IN OUR FIELD?
- WHERE DO WE WANT TO BE IN 2030?
- WHAT CHALLENGES ARE WE FACING?

	PROCESS-ORIENTED	RESULT-ORIENTED	SUBJECT-ORIENTED
BROAD QUESTIONS	HOW MIGHT WE IMPROVE THIS PROCESS?	HOW WOULD OTHERS LOOK AT THIS RESULT?	WHY DO WE NEED TO CHANGE?
	WHAT WAS THE BEST PART OF THIS WORKSHOP?	WHO WILL BENEFIT FROM THIS OUTCOME? / WHAT CAN SUPPORT OR CHALLENGE THIS RESULT?	WHO ARE OUR MAIN STAKEHOLDERS? / WHAT WOULD OUR CUSTOMERS SAY?
NARROW QUESTIONS	ARE WE ON THE RIGHT TRACK?	WILL OUR RESULT MAKE SENSE FOR OTHERS?	DO WE HAVE WHAT IT TAKES?
BRAINSTORM	HOW DO WE PREPARE FOR THIS?	WHAT IS THE BIGGER PURPOSE OF THIS WORK?	WHO IS RESPONSIBLE FOR WHAT? / WHAT WILL IT TAKE TO DO THIS?

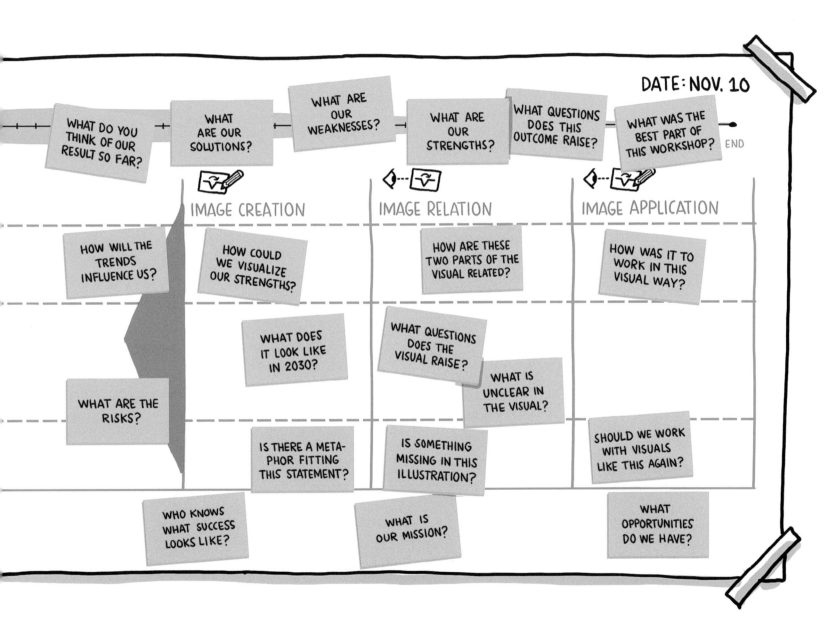

Summary

Good questions promote dialogue. A good question serves as an overture to examine, explore, and discover together.

A large part of a facilitator's professional skills resides in the ability to ask good questions.

Good process questions support the purpose of the process, advance the process toward its goal, and ensure that concrete results are generated that can be used going forward.

We divide our questions into two categories: facilitation questions and visualization questions.

Facilitation questions:

– Subject-oriented

– Results-oriented

– Process-oriented

Visualization questions:

– Image creation

– Image relation

– Image application

Question Designer

Get an overview of all your questions using the Question Designer.

WHAT QUESTIONS WOULD BE
VALUABLE TO ASK EVERYONE
IN YOUR ORGANIZATION?

A compass for good decision making

Copenhagen Metro and Greater Copenhagen Light Rail underwent a major transformation in just a few short years, from being an organization of 50 primarily Danish employees to being an organization of 300 employees of many nationalities. They also went from being a project organization to being a matrix organization. In other words, their internal complexity increased significantly and the need for a common understanding of roles and responsibilities became necessary. The organization's public ownership is of major significance to how the organization develops and how decisions are made.

The management group needed to give employees a clear picture of how decisions are made and what types of decisions should be made where.

The management group therefore wanted to have a tool that could handle dialogue in the various units, addressing questions such as:

— Who are we? (What type of company are we?)
— What is a matrix organization?
— How do we make good decisions?
— What forums meet when and what decisions belong to which forums?

At the same time, the tool needed to help employees at all levels of the organization navigate everyday decisions.

For many years, several members of the management group had used a model to guide their employees in making good decisions. In an enlarged and visual version, this model became a central part of the dialogue tool using eight questions, so it could guide a decision-making process.

Decision-making compass:
During the design process, the model was expanded with additional questions and made visual. If a given employee answered no to one or more of the eight questions, the decision was no longer one he or she should make on their own.

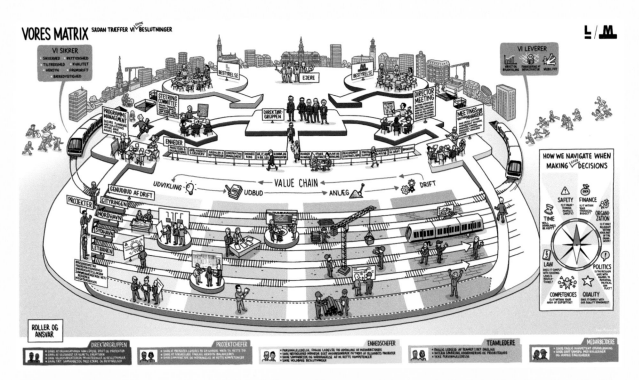

Dialogue tool: The structure of the dialogue tool was built around the company's own organizational chart together with a reference to their circular value chain. The tool was later presented and adjusted by managers, team leaders, and division managers to make sure that they owned the tool and would be able to facilitate valuable dialogues in their units.

4.
Create engaging templates

CREATE ENGAGING TEMPLATES

PURPOSE: TO OFFER A RECIPE FOR
HOW TO DESIGN TEMPLATES

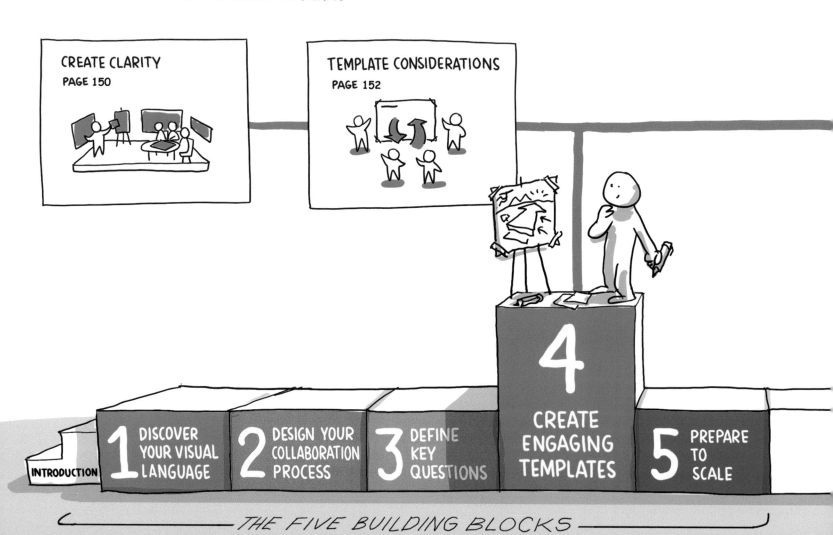

CREATE CLARITY
PAGE 150

TEMPLATE CONSIDERATIONS
PAGE 152

INTRODUCTION

1 DISCOVER YOUR VISUAL LANGUAGE

2 DESIGN YOUR COLLABORATION PROCESS

3 DEFINE KEY QUESTIONS

4 CREATE ENGAGING TEMPLATES

5 PREPARE TO SCALE

THE FIVE BUILDING BLOCKS

GOAL: YOU HAVE A TEMPLATE THAT WILL CREATE VALUE IN YOUR NEXT MEETING, PROJECT, OR PROCESS

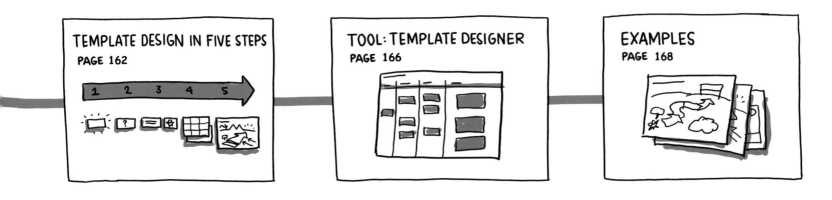

TEMPLATE DESIGN IN FIVE STEPS
PAGE 162

1 2 3 4 5

TOOL: TEMPLATE DESIGNER
PAGE 166

EXAMPLES
PAGE 168

6 ENABLE GROUP LEARNING

7 MAP YOUR SKILLS

8 ACTIVATE YOUR RESOURCES

9 DO'S & DON'TS

Create clarity

Why templates? A template organizes information visually. A template can provide a framework and create clarity in a process in sections or as a whole. Good templates can handle complexity, focus dialogues, and promote collective learning.

Templates must be adapted to fit the situation; they must be based on the purpose of the process and make use of (some of) your pre-designed process questions.

BUILD YOUR LEARNING ARENA

When you work visually, it makes sense to use the physical surfaces of the room to chart information and structure dialogues. We call this building a visual learning arena. You will find it to your advantage to build your visual learning arena from templates. Your learning arena needs to support your participants in working in a structured, holistic, and systematic manner with their shared knowledge. Each template can be used to frame one element in your process design. Each template has its own purpose, but together the templates all serve the overarching purpose and goal of a given process. Start small. Create a simple template that supports a single part of your process design.

Examples: Here are six templates that each frame a process step in a workshop.

WORKSHOP AGENDA

A template presenting participants with the workshop's purpose and goals, and the day's program.

MIND MAP

A template with one important question and room to list and draw participant responses.

TIMELINE

A template with a timeline can be used to review important events and trends over time.

PROCESS MAPPING

A template with room for sticky notes, allowing participants to map out what an optimal process might look like.

GROUP DIALOGUE

The group works with a subject by answering questions in a template. There is room to write and draw the group's response on the template.

REFLECTION CARD

A card with a question and space to enter an answer.

Template considerations

When you are developing a template, you must decide whether it will be used to support a dialogue or to present knowledge. A template can also be designed as a combined dialogue and presentation tool.

Dialogue or presentation? In choosing whether to develop a dialogue tool or a presentation tool, several parameters come into play: What is the tool's purpose? What situation will it be used in? What is the subject? Who will use it? The overarching considerations in relation to your overall process design are all important here, even if for the moment you are only developing a tool for use in a small part of the process. Here are a few guidelines that can help direct your choice:

Create a dialogue tool when:

– Your participants' knowledge needs to come into play.
– There is a need to structure and focus a dialogue.
– Your participants need to feel that they are seen and heard.

Create a combination tool when:

– You need both to communicate important information to a group, and…
– You have time or space for a structured dialogue where your participants' knowledge can come into play.
– It is important that your participants feel their input is needed.

Create a presentation tool when:

– The purpose of the template is to communicate a large amount of new information to a group.
– Facts must be presented.
– There is little time or space for dialogue.

Whatever tool you aim to create, it is good to start with your questions formulated in the previous building block. What questions will be included in this template? Do any of the questions need to be answered in advance? Do all questions require input from your participants?

Behind any presentation tool lies a dialogue tool: a number of questions that have already been answered. Once completed, any dialogue tool can therefore become a presentation tool. Once the series of questions has been answered and visualized, the tool is ready to be used for a presentation.

The visualizations to the right show the difference between a dialogue tool and a presentation tool. In the middle you see a combination of the two.

VISUAL DIALOGUE TOOL

A visual dialogue tool is a template with text, graphs, and illustrations that structure a group's dialogue around a set of questions. The dialogue can be facilitated by a facilitator, but the dialogue tool can also be designed to support a group's own facilitation.

VISUAL PRESENTATION AND DIALOGUE TOOL

A combined presentation and dialogue tool is a template that both communicates information and asks questions. Parts of the template's contents are entered in advance, and parts are filled in along the way.

VISUAL PRESENTATION TOOL

A visual presentation tool is a template with text, figures, and illustrations that communicates information. The group's task is primarily to listen and understand. The template is often designed in advance and does not change along the way. The template often has an owner who presents its content.

TEMPLATE CONSIDERATIONS

Here you see an example of what an organizational strategy can look like when it changes from a dialogue tool to a presentation tool.

| DIALOGUE TOOL | PRESENTATION AND DIALOGUE TOOL |

Here is a template to structure a strategic dialogue. All four questions are to be answered by the participants.

Here the participants are presented with "Where we are today!" The participants must find answers to the remaining three parts of the strategy.

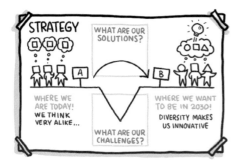

The template shows "Where we are" and "Where we are headed." The participants must find their own answers to "What challenges are we facing?" and "What solutions do we see?"

Here the participants are presented with three main messages that will prompt them to respond to the single question of the template: "What solutions do we see?"

The template is used to present the strategy and answer all the questions, including "Where are we?" "Where are we headed?" "What challenges are we facing?" and "How do we solve them?"

TEMPLATE CONSIDERATIONS

Structure

A structure is the underlying skeleton that brings all your template elements together as a whole. The visual structure refers to the visual elements you use, a bit like when you are designing a PowerPoint slide show and creating boxes, lines, and speech bubbles to create a good flow and a good balance in your presentation. The visual structure in your templates helps your process participants see connections, and understand the whole. A good structure makes your content easy to present, easy to understand, and logical to work with.

Keep the structure simple in your first templates. A chronological layout is easy to work with.

Design your learning arena to be as simple as possible. Put your content on flip charts—one by one in the sequence in which they will be used. Or, if you have plenty of wall space, draw your templates on a large landscape-format sheet and place it on the wall.

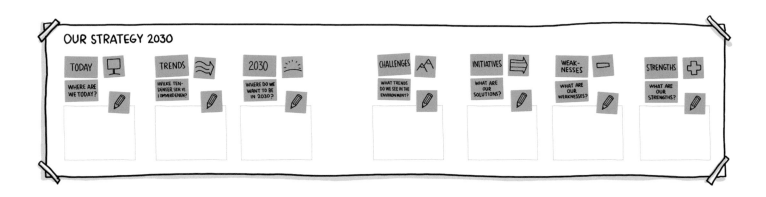

SCHEMATIC STRUCTURE

A schematic structure is a combination of basic shapes: lines, squares, circles, triangles, and arrows. The possibilities for combination are infinite. Let the content determine what shapes work best for your template, and their number and size.

HOW?

The most basic shapes can accommodate large amounts of information and complexity—an entire organization's structure with roles and responsibilities, a value chain from production to delivery or a relevant pie chart from the company's annual reports. Combine and support your narrative or dialogue with:

– Circles coinciding to show overlap between knowledge areas, organizational units, or groups
– Triangles or squares coinciding to show parts of a whole
– Tables to show different units compared against one another
– Squares, circles, and boxes to show foundations, columns, or buildings
– Or any other geometric variations that suggest ideas

STRENGTHS

Basic shapes communicate in a matter-of-fact manner and are not as subject to misinterpretation or overinterpretation as metaphors can be. Schematic diagrams are used in many different contexts, and we are therefore used to decoding them.

WEAKNESSES

Some shapes are used to such an extent that they become invisible or boring. We stop "reading" them because we think we know the content.

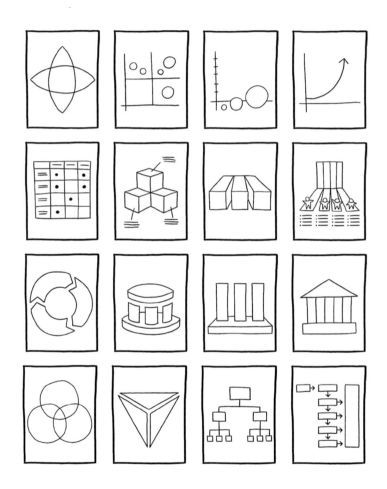

METAPHORICAL

A metaphor is a linguistic image. A visual metaphor is a drawing of a linguistic image and it can be used as a coherent structure for your template.

Let your content determine the linguistic image. Your metaphor must follow the content visually.

HOW?

Bring life to your narrative by letting yourself be inspired by visual metaphors that fit your subject. Think about travel, nature, transportation, sports, or leisure.

– Use a tree to have a conversation about the roots, trunk, leaves, and fruits of a project
– An iceberg could lead to dialogue about the visible and invisible
– A juggler evokes prioritization of work tasks
– Mountain climbing might suggest dialogues about collaboration or performance

STRENGTHS

Metaphors can generate new insights and ideas. They can broaden perspective on a subject and reveal fresh angles. They can make abstract subjects concrete, so they are easy to recognize and recall.

WEAKNESSES

Some metaphors are so overused that they are perceived as cliché. Others may be effective in speech, but may come across as childish or inappropriate when depicted visually. Metaphors can also distract, such as when the entire staff of an organization gets caught up in talking about the details of the art of mountaineering instead of the actual content of their strategy just because they were presented with a mountain climbing metaphor.

TEMPLATE CONSIDERATIONS

Size, form, and function

What is the right format for your template, and does it need to have a special function? It may seem banal, but the shape and size of your template can be of vital importance for how your tool works in practice. Shape and size can help determine how and to what extent your participants can be involved.

You should choose your format on the basis of both physical constraints and what best supports the purpose of the template and the desired results. How will the template be presented to the participants? How will they work with it? Also consider the function of the template; for example, does it need to be able to fit into a conference packet or perhaps be divided in half during the process?

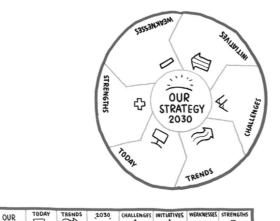

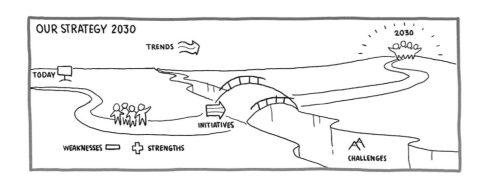

SIZE AND SHAPE

The size and shape of your template should depend on the process, the purpose, and the desired results. Physical frameworks can, however, also dictate the design of the template in advance. In the general sense, small templates work best for small groups of three to five people, and large templates work best for larger groups who need to see and work in a panoramic format. Make it easy; use standard formats or other formats that have already been used in your organization. If you have room in your budget, use surprising shapes adapt a group template to the shape of the conference table—alternative sizes and shapes can spark creativity and prepare the ground for innovative solutions.

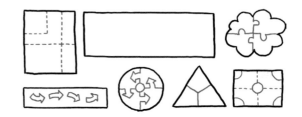

FUNCTION

Consider what function best fits your template's process, purpose, and goals. Do your participants need to have a personal copy of the template and to reflect on their own before group work? Do they need to carry answers from one stage into another? Or will they need to send an answer to a colleague on the other side of the world? Don't let yourself be limited by time and space. Experiment with the function of your template and consider whether elements need to be folded, shared, cut out, or joined.

Template design in five steps

Developing good templates takes time; on the other hand, they can often be reused and with a few minor adjustments adapted to new projects or topics. This building block has five steps that can help you develop a template.

If you have developed a visual language, a process design, and a series of questions on the subject your template will be exploring, use these.

Consider whether you can work in the final format from the beginning, because it gives a good sense for size constraints, hierarchies, parts, and wholes.

1. TITLE

Give your template a title that presents the subject of the template.

Why?
A title offers focus and direction in both the development and use of a template.

How?
A good title should answer the question: "What is this?" Come up with a few options and then choose the best title. Consider whether or how the title appeals to your participants.

Test
Is your title attention-grabbing? Does it inspire? Does it engage? Or does it at least get noticed?

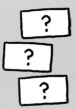
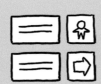

2. QUESTIONS

Arrange your template questions in a sequence. Select the questions that you will be using in your template. Place them in prioritized sequence.

Why?
In the previous building block we showed why it is important to work with questions and how to use the Question Designer. If you have created a series of questions for your process, now you can select the questions to be included in your template.

How?
List your questions in the sequence in which they need to be presented.

Test
Use the question test and the process diamond from the previous building block.

3. HEADING AND ICON

Create a header and an icon for each question.

Why?
Supporting visualizations help your participants understand your questions. They can emphasize details and prevent misunderstandings.

How?
Write a heading for each question and use the Eighth Element method from the first building block to create icons.

Test
Invite your colleagues to provide feedback.

4. PROTOTYPING

Use the elements created in step 3. Experiment with size, shape, function, and structure. Design one or more prototypes of your template.

Why?
Prototypes let you test your way forward to the best solution.

How?
Work with sticky notes so the elements from step 3 can be shifted around. Create space for your participants' replies. Use empty sticky notes to get a sense of space. Remember to clarify the sequence of the questions if your template needs to function without facilitation.

Test
Take two steps back and choose the prototype that is the most balanced and comprehensible.

5. DRAW

After choosing the best prototype, find paper of the right size and shape, create a frame, and draw gridlines in a light color. This makes it easier to organize your content and work with size restraints. Draw the template.

Template elements

Here is an overview of elements to keep in mind when designing a template.

The strategy template to the right was developed for a management group that needed a structured dialogue around their strategy. In building block 2 you can find the associated process design; in block 1, the icons; and in block 3, the questions. This strategy template is just one example of how you can build a template.

We recommend that you:

– *Work with prototypes:* Test your way forward to the best solution. You can make additions or take things out. Organize your template according to the content. It's not always the first solution that serves your purpose best.
– *Acknowledge that it takes time:* It also takes time to create a good PowerPoint presentation. Decide how much time you intend to spend and maintain focus along the way.
– *Make it reader-friendly:* Maintain solid logic in your template so it becomes reader-friendly, even at a distance. Consider reading direction, hierarchies, text sizes, and fonts. Too much back and forth makes the viewer restless.

AND DON'T FORGET

Use the Seven Elements
Show people, places, processes, speech, text, colors, and effects.

Include your name and date
Show who created the template and indicate the date. Templates are rarely static.

Frame
Delimit and frame content.

Blank spaces
To create calm.

Cohesive visual structure
Binds the content together into a unified picture—chronologically, schematically, meta-phorically, or in combination.

SEQUENCE

Work with the sequence of the elements so the template is easy to decode when it is transferred to the big screen.

TITLE

Short and attention-grabbing title that gives focus and direction.

RESPONSE FIELDS

Blank fields with room to write or draw the participants' replies.

HEADINGS

Brief headings that contain the essence of your process questions.

CORE QUESTIONS

Complete but brief sentences that are easy to understand and recall. The phrases must be based on your participants and unambiguously formulated. The core questions can be left out if use of the template is facilitated.

ICONS

Use icons from your visual language to support title, headings, and questions.

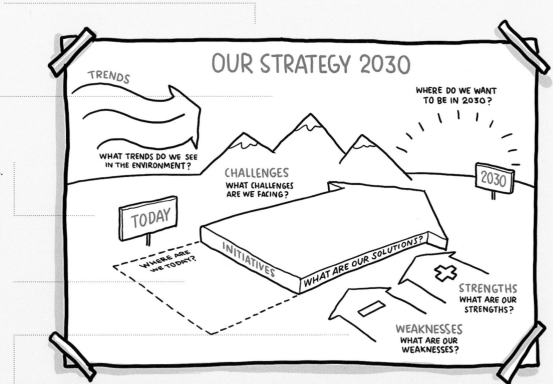

FORM, SIZE, AND FUNCTION

Consider the shape, size, and function in relation to the purpose of the template and the physical frameworks of the process situation.

TOOL

Template Designer

Use the Template Designer when you work your way through the five steps. Download and print or draw the tool.

HOW?

Work with the Template Designer from left to right. Once you have decided upon your finished template, draw it in 1:1 on a new piece of paper.

STICKY NOTES/PAPER

Use rectangular sticky notes when working with titles, questions, and headings.

Use square sticky notes for your icons.

Use 8½" × 11" sheets or large sticky notes for your prototypes.

 Download the Template Designer on www.visualcollaboration.site.

TEMPLATE DESIGNER

TEMPLATE DESIGN FOR:_____

DATE:_____

BY :_____

TITLE [TITLE]   QUESTIONS [?][?][?]   HEADING & ICON   PROTOTYPING

CONSIDERATIONS: DIALOGUE/ PRESENTATION   STRUCTURE   SIZE   FORM   FUNCTION

TEMPLATE DESIGNER

TEMPLATE DESIGN FOR: Strategy workshop

DATE: _____

BY: _____

TITLE : TITLE   QUESTIONS ?   HEADING & ICON   PROTOTYPING

OUR STRATEGY 2030

WHERE ARE WE TODAY? — TODAY 🖥️

WHAT TRENDS DO WE SEE IN THE ENVIRONMENT? — TRENDS 〰️

WHERE DO WE WANT TO BE IN 2030? — 2030 ☀️

WHAT CHALLENGES ARE WE FACING? — CHALLENGES ⛰️

WHAT ARE OUR SOLUTIONS? — INITIATIVES ➡️

WHAT ARE OUR WEAKNESSES? — WEAK-NESSES ▭

WHAT ARE OUR STRENGTHS? — STRENGTHS ✚

OUR STRATEGY 2030 — **Chronological**

OUR STRATEGY 2030 — **Schematic**

OUR STRATEGY 2030 — **Metaphorical**

CONSIDERATIONS: DIALOGUE/PRESENTATION   STRUCTURE   SIZE   FORM   FUNCTION

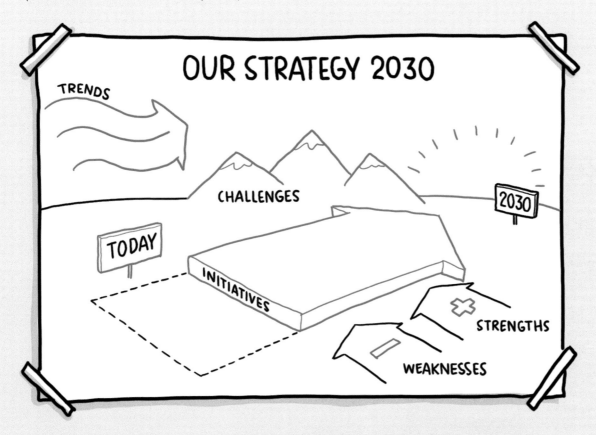

A strategy can be difficult to make concrete and usable and there is sometimes a gap between an organization's strategy and the work employees perform. The strategy template can make strategy work practical and action-oriented, regardless of what type of organization it is used in.

Purpose: To provide a structured and action-oriented dialogue with relevant stakeholders on the organization's upcoming or current strategy. The participants use the seven questions to the left to approach the broad strokes of the strategy. The template is filled in with responses on sticky notes, so the process is flexible, and the responses can be changed or shifted around when new insights arise.

Download Our Strategy 2030 on www.visualcollaboration.site.

TOOL   EXAMPLES

TEMPLATE DESIGNER

TEMPLATE DESIGN FOR: _Meeting agenda_

DATE: _____

BY: _____

TITLE	QUESTIONS	HEADING & ICON	PROTOTYPING

TITLE: AGENDA

QUESTIONS:
- WHAT IS THE PURPOSE OF THE MEETING?
- WHAT IS THE GOAL OF THE MEETING?
- WHAT ARE THE RESULTS OF THE MEETING?
- WHO ARE THE PARTICIPANTS IN THE MEETING?
- WHAT ARE THE AGENDA ITEMS OF THE MEETING?
- WHAT PRINCIPLES WILL GUIDE THE MEETING?
- WHAT ARE THE NEXT STEPS AFTER THE MEETING?
- WHAT ARE THE CHECK-IN QUESTIONS?

HEADING & ICON:
- PURPOSE
- GOAL
- RESULTS
- PARTICI-PANTS
- AGENDA
- PRINCIPLES
- NEXT STEPS
- CHECK-IN QUESTIONS

PROTOTYPING:

AGENDA — **Chronological**

AGENDA — **Schematic**

AGENDA — **Metaphorical**

CONSIDERATIONS: DIALOGUE/PRESENTATION   STRUCTURE   SIZE   FORM   FUNCTION

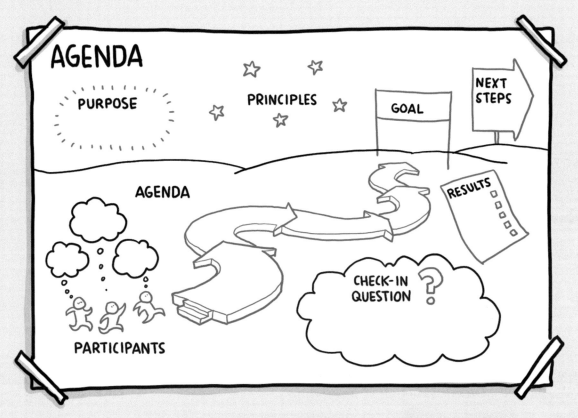

A visual agenda is an engaging and easy way to present a meeting, workshop, or conference.

Purpose: To explain to a group of participants what meeting they will be attending. A visual agenda can be constructed according to the eight questions to the left. The eight questions are not only about the program points of the meeting, but also about the meeting's purpose, goals, and principles that will ensure that the participants are on target with the results of the meeting. The template also has room so the meeting participants can answer a question at the start of the meeting.

Download the Meeting Agenda on www.visualcollaboration.site.

TOOL EXAMPLES

TEMPLATE DESIGNER

TEMPLATE DESIGN FOR: Business model generation

DATE: _____

BY: _____

TITLE [TITLE]   QUESTIONS [?]   HEADING & ICON   PROTOTYPING

TITLE	QUESTIONS	HEADING & ICON
BUSINESS MODEL	WHO ARE OUR MOST IMPORTANT CUSTOMER SEGMENTS?	CUSTOMER SEGMENTS
	WHAT VALUE DO WE CREATE FOR THE CUSTOMER?	VALUE CREATION
	THROUGH WHAT CHANNELS DO WE REACH THE CUSTOMER?	CHANNELS
	WHAT IS OUR RELATIONSHIP WITH THE CUSTOMER?	CUSTOMER RELATIONSHIPS
	WHAT REVENUE STREAMS DO WE HAVE?	REVENUE STREAM
	WHAT KEY RESOURCES ARE NECESSARY?	KEY RESOURCES
	WHAT KEY ACTIVITIES ARE NECESSARY?	KEY ACTIVITIES
	WHO ARE OUR MOST IMPORTANT PARTNERS?	KEY PARTNERS
	WHERE ARE THE MOST SIGNIFICANT COSTS?	COST STRUCTURE

PROTOTYPING

BUSINESS MODEL — **Chronological**

BUSINESS MODEL — **Schematic**

BUSINESS MODEL — **Metaphorical**

CONSIDERATIONS: DIALOGUE/PRESENTATION   STRUCTURE   SIZE   FORM   FUNCTION

Template by Alexander Osterwalder and Yves Pigneur
(Schematic) The chronological and metaphorical prototypes are our suggestions of
how the template might have also looked.

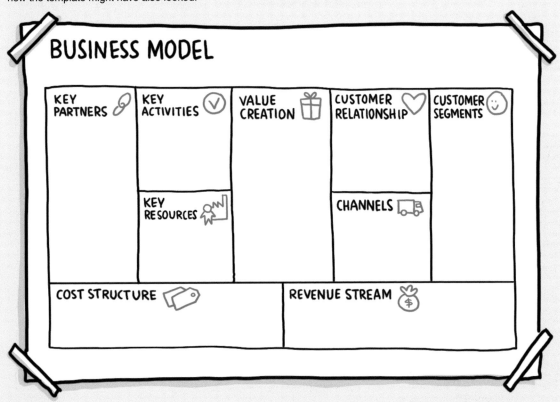

In 2010 Alexander Osterwalder and Yves Pigneur released the book *Business Model Generation*. It included a visual dialogue tool called "Business Model Canvas."

Business Model Generation is about how you can develop new business models or update existing ones.

The book introduces nine core questions that guide you and your group through a focused dialogue about your business model. The nine questions each have their own icons that are entered into the template. The template has room for sticky notes in each field so you and your group can flexibly discuss and prioritize your answers.

The book, the method, and the tool have become a global success.

Alexander Osterwalder and
Yves Pigneur
Visit strategyzer.com, download the tool, invite interested parties, and create, revisit, and test your next business model together.

Templates you may know

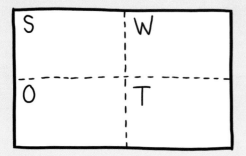

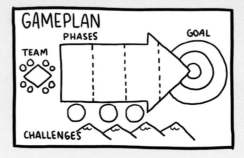

SWOT

Analyze the Strengths, Weaknesses, Opportunities, and Threats of a business or project, and create a better foundation to make decisions.

Unknown origin

GAMEPLAN

Use a gameplan to get an overview of your next project. Invite your project participants into a process where you clarify your roles, break the project into phases, map out challenges, and formulate goals.

David Sibbet
The Grove Consultants International

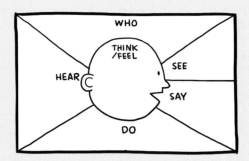

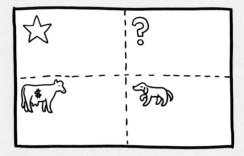

EMPATHY MAP

Explore user profiles by mapping the behavior of various profiles. Choose a person and analyze what they hear, think, feel, see, say, and do.

Dave Gray
Xplane

BOSTON MATRIX

Analyze your company's products by looking at market shares and growth potential. The purpose of this template is to identify what products are the most profitable. Categorize the products as cash cows, dead dogs, question marks, or stars.

Boston Consulting Group

Inspiration

Here is a selection of templates, in simplified form, that we have developed
for various purposes for a wide array of different organizations.
Visit visualcollaboration.site for more ideas.

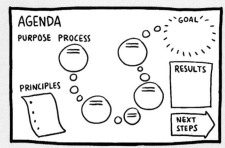

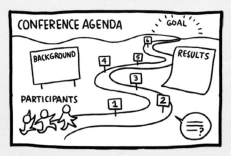

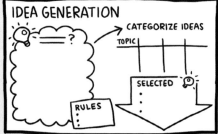

Summary

Create clarity: A good template can handle complexity, focus dialogues, and promote collective learning. You construct your visual learning arena from templates that can help you and your participants work with a holistic perspective and reach results in less time.

Template considerations: When you develop a template, you must consider whether it needs to support a presentation or dialogue; if the structure must be chronological, schematic, or metaphorical; and what size and form best supports the function of the template.

Template design: You can develop templates in five steps:

– Formulate title

– Arrange questions in sequence

– Create headings and icons

– Design prototypes

– Draw

Template Designer: A tool that helps you structure your design process when you are developing a template.

Examples: There are many existing templates you can use for inspiration and adapt to your own situations and processes.

WHAT IS THE TITLE OF
YOUR NEXT TEMPLATE?

The big picture of purchasing

IKEA is a global organization that often works with procedures and manuals in order to ensure quality and uniform deliveries. IKEA Purchasing & Logistics is no exception to this.

For many years they had been using a 30-page manual describing the unit's work in detail. The content of the manual was nonetheless interpreted very differently from one office to another around the world. In order to create a common understanding and uniform sense of direction, groups from each office met for a series of workshops with the objective of developing a common picture of Purchasing & Logistics.

Over the course of many workshops, the participants received training in developing a visual language based on their common manual and local experiences. Sketches from the initial workshops were analyzed, developed, and used in a follow-up calibration workshop, in which the visual work from the initial workshops was compiled into a single drawing and submitted for approval among key employees. Finally, this drawing was freshly redone by an illustrator.

The Big Picture of Purchasing was formulated, drawn, commented on, edited, and rearranged by more than 100 employees at IKEA. Since the first finished version, it has been updated five times. Today, it is used daily by more than 2,000 employees in IKEA Purchasing & Logistics. It's been hung up in hallways and offices, and is available on IKEA's intranet as an interactive tool where employees can click through different levels of detail. It is also used as a dialogue tool in workshops focusing on ways to improve purchasing and thus serves as part of the onboarding process for new employees.

Example of a sketch created by a group of employees for one of the first workshops.

A larger visualization created by merging sketches from the initial workshops.

The final drawing before being redone by an illustrator.

"Today, anyone who needs to know anything about the Supplier Life Cycle in Purchasing & Logistics can use the image to navigate through our complexity. The visual aspect shortens the time it takes to find the information you need and makes it much easier to remember the content. Since we started using the poster, we've gone through three major organizational changes. The picture has remained more or less unchanged and is still a cornerstone of our work, regardless of how we are structured."

Henrik Elm
Purchasing & Logistics Manager,
Inter IKEA Group

The final poster, 5th version

The layout of the drawing: The customer is seen at the center surrounded by a ring of strategies. Eight interconnected processes compose the centermost ring. The outermost ring shows the entire IKEA process from customer need to customer satisfaction. It is all based on IKEA's foundation, which is made up of five core documents.

5.
Prepare to scale

PREPARE TO SCALE

PURPOSE: TO INSPIRE YOU TO WORK VISUALLY WHEN SCALING YOUR PROCESSES

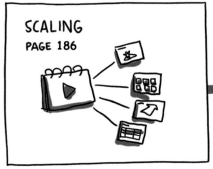

SCALING
PAGE 186

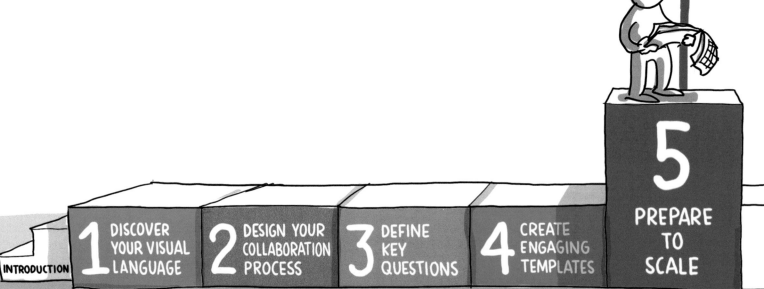

INTRODUCTION

1 DISCOVER YOUR VISUAL LANGUAGE

2 DESIGN YOUR COLLABORATION PROCESS

3 DEFINE KEY QUESTIONS

4 CREATE ENGAGING TEMPLATES

5 PREPARE TO SCALE

THE FIVE BUILDING BLOCKS

GOAL: YOU HAVE A PLAYBOOK ENABLING OTHERS TO SCALE YOUR WORK

THE VISUAL PLAYBOOK
PAGE 188

TOOL: PLAYBOOK DESIGNER
PAGE 198

6 ENABLE GROUP LEARNING

7 MAP YOUR SKILLS

8 ACTIVATE YOUR RESOURCES

9 DO'S & DON'TS

Scaling

Why playbooks? A playbook is a tool that shows in detail what needs to happen in a process. This is particularly relevant to processes that need to be facilitated by others, and when large and complex processes with many stakeholders and high stakes are involved.

In working with the Process Designer in building block 2, you entered the key data points of:

– The situation in which the process will be taking place
– Each process step
– The process results
– The next step of the process.

In your visual playbook you describe and visualize these elements in greater detail. It is these that, together with a detailed schedule, constitute the elements of your visual playbook.

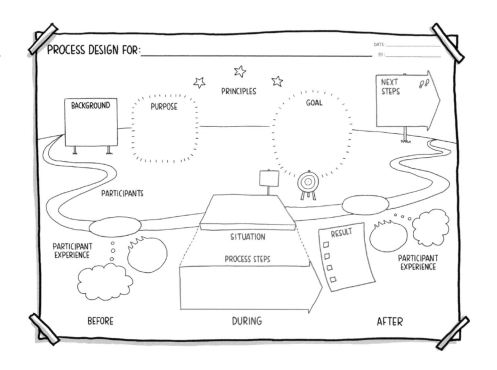

186

A good playbook provides *freedom and flexibility, ownership,* and *space for improvisation.*

– If you are responsible for designing, facilitating, or running a large-scale conference where a lot is at stake, and there are many roles and responsibilities to fill, the playbook provides a strong foundation to work from.

– If you have designed a meeting concept or a change process that will be rolled out to your entire organization, the playbook is a great tool to increase the likelihood that others will be successful with your design.

– If you are part of an organization that is not used to working visually, the development of a playbook can help you stay two steps ahead when you need to involve your participants in drawing or using a template.

The visual playbook

Work with the four design elements in the sequence and depth that work best for you and your process.

SKETCH THE SITUATION

Sketch the situation in which the process is taking place.

VISUALIZE THE ANTICIPATED RESULTS

Sketch what the anticipated results look like.

STORYBOARD

Create a storyboard illustrating each process step before, during, and after.

SCHEDULE

Create a schedule that follows the storyboard and describes each process step in detail.

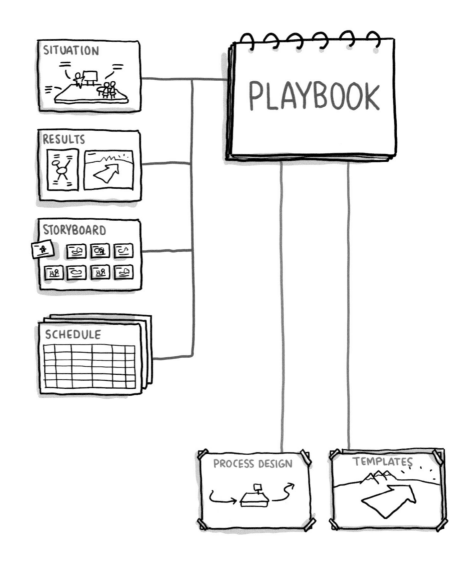

THE VISUAL PLAYBOOK

Sketch the situation

Draw a sketch of the situation that forms the framework of the process.

WHY?

By outlining the situation in which the process will be taking place, you and others involved in the process will have an overview of the concept of the process. The sketch can reveal whether anything is missing or if there are other things you need to consider to be able to run the process.

HOW?

Draw your learning arena: seating arrangement, scene, equipment, and materials. Draw the participants and their various roles, responsibilities, and tasks. Describe the concept of the process in a short sentence. Include the sketch in your playbook.

190

SITUATION

BRIEF INTRODUCTION TO STRATEGY FROM EXECUTIVE BOARD MEMBERS FOLLOWED BY GROUP WORK ON STRATEGY USING THE GROUP TEMPLATE

TIME
2 HOURS
OCTOBER 10

PARTICIPANTS
ROLES/RESPONSIBILITIES/TASKS

PLACE
BOARDROOM

SETUP & EQUIPMENT
2 GROUP TABLES
(CLOSE TOGETHER)

FACILITATOR:
– CONDUCTS PROCESS
– MAKES VISUAL SUMMARIES ALONG THE WAY (WHITEBOARD)

PARTICIPANTS:
– 2 EXECUTIVE BOARD MEMBERS: BRIEF FRAMING
– 10 TOP MANAGERS: DISCUSS, REFLECT, WRITE & DRAW (STICKY NOTES)

MATERIALS
– TAPE
– STICKY NOTES
– MARKERS (2 SETS)
– WHITEBOARD MARKERS

– 1 GROUP TEMPLATE (ON WALL, 90×150CM)
– 1 WHITEBOARD FOR SHARED NOTES

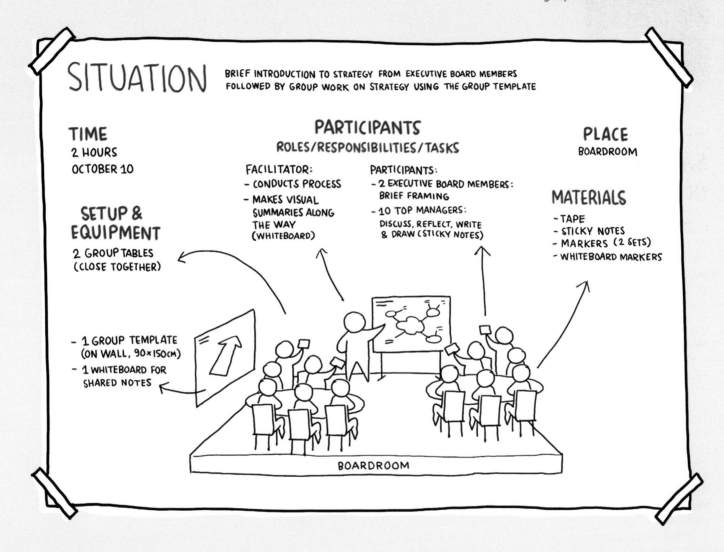

BOARDROOM

191

THE VISUAL PLAYBOOK

Visualize the anticipated results

Draw your expectations of the process results.

WHY?

By visualizing the desired results of the process you are increasing the chances of success. You make the results of the process concrete and achievable and may discover that something needs to be changed in order to achieve your goals.

When the desired result is visible to you, it is also easier to describe how to proceed.

HOW?

When you work visually, there are often one or more visual end products in the form of completed templates, whiteboards, or flip charts.

Visualize what you imagine the participants have produced, or what will be drawn up on the walls or whiteboards once your process is completed.

Include sketches of the desired results in the playbook.

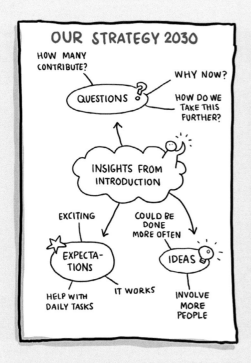

Flip chart – End result:
10 to 20 ideas and insights drawn
up on a flip chart

Template – End result:
Prioritized answers to each
question

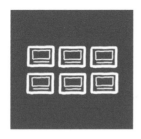

THE VISUAL PLAYBOOK

Storyboard

Draw the process steps before, during, and after.

WHY?

A good storyboard is clear about all key process steps. It provides overview and control of your process and is a valuable tool for ensuring a good delivery. A storyboard is also a tool for knowledge sharing about, and improvement of, your process design.

HOW?

Break your process down into steps. Create a new step and a new frame each time you have a "scene change." Make each scene movable so you can experiment with the sequence. Give each scene a number, a title, a time indicator, and a brief description of content. Sketch the key points of what is going on. What does it look like?

Remember to show both the steps of the process itself, and also what needs to be done before and after, so that your learning arena works, and it is clear to your contributors how the results created will be carried forward. Include the storyboard in your playbook.

Before

During

BRIEFING   30 MIN

SHORT REVIEW: PROCESS
+ SEND OUT INVITE

SET UP ROOM   30 MIN

FACILITATOR SETS UP
EQUIPMENT & MATERIALS

PARTICIPANTS ARE   10 MIN
INVITED IN

FACILITATOR & MANAGER: PARTICI-
PANTS ARE EXPECTED + WELCOME

INTRODUCTION   5 MIN

MANAGER WELCOMES EVERYONE
+ EXPLAINS THE PROCESS

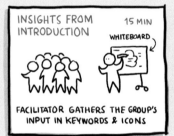

INSIGHTS FROM   15 MIN
INTRODUCTION

WHITEBOARD

FACILITATOR GATHERS THE GROUP'S
INPUT IN KEYWORDS & ICONS

INDIVIDUAL REFLECTION   15 MIN

STICKY
NOTES

PARTICIPANTS WRITE OWN ANSWERS TO
4 CORE QUESTIONS FROM THE FACILITATOR

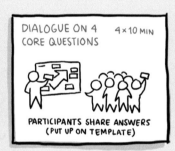

DIALOGUE ON 4   4×10 MIN
CORE QUESTIONS

PARTICIPANTS SHARE ANSWERS
(PUT UP ON TEMPLATE)

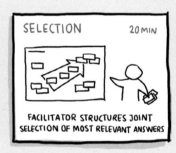

SELECTION   20 MIN

FACILITATOR STRUCTURES JOINT
SELECTION OF MOST RELEVANT ANSWERS

After

RECAP: 20 MIN
QUESTIONS & PROCESS

GROUP DRAWS THE FINAL
ANSWERS DIRECTLY ON TEMPLATE

CONCLUSION &   10 MIN
NEXT STEPS

MANAGER WRAP UP +
"THANK YOU FOR PARTICIPATING"

DOCUMENTATION   10 MIN
& SHARING

FACILITATOR TAKES PHOTOS
& SHARES WITH PARTICIPANTS

PROCESSING OF   60 MIN
INPUT

FACILITATOR & MANAGER COMPILE

THE VISUAL PLAYBOOK

Schedule

Create a detailed schedule of the entire process.

WHY?

A schedule is a classic facilitation tool. This tool makes your process actionable and ensures that all contributors provide their contributions at the right time and in the right form. You should not be a slave to your schedule, but once you are well-prepared in detail, you also know what is happening if you need to change something in the execution.

HOW?

Create a text document with the points you find relevant. Remember to use your answers from the Process Designer. These answers have guided you in the development of your process, and they will also guide you and your contributors in the delivery.

In addition to the fields for time, title, content, activity, responsibility, comment, and materials, it can also be a good idea for the schedule to include a field with an illustration of what a process step looks like. Cut and paste elements of your storyboard or show the template that will be used in the step in question. Include the schedule in your playbook.

Schedule: Strategy workshop. Monday 10 October, 9:00-11:00 AM.

Start	Time Minutes	Heading	Content (purpose & activity)	Person(s) responsible	Comments	Materials	Illustrations
BEFORE							
1 week prior	00:30	Briefing and sending out of invitation	Facilitator and members of the Executive Board conduct a brief review of the process. Invitation is sent to participants.	Facilitator		Template, text for agenda, invitation	
8:20 AM	00:30	Setup	The premises are arranged for 2 groups, each of 5 participants with materials ready.	Facilitator	Everyone must be able to see the template. Draw up an agenda.	Template, 1 whiteboard, box of materials, including markers and sticky notes	
08:50 AM	00:10	Ready for participants to be invited in	Show the participants that they are expected and welcome. The premises should be ready and inviting.	Executive members + Facilitator	Provide name cards	Coffee, tea, breakfast, fresh air	
DURING							
09:00 AM	00:05	Introduction to workshop	Welcome. Introduction to purpose, process, and the desired results of the strategy workshop.	Executive members + Facilitator	Print template and questions for each participant.	Template	
09:05 AM	00:15	Insights from the introduction	What insights did the introduction provide? Compiling of the participants' insights from the introduction in key terms and icons on whiteboard.	Facilitator	Use color codes for input.	Whiteboard and markers	
09:20 AM	00:10	Individual reflection	Have everyone consider the 4 core questions. All participants note their own responses on sticky notes.	Facilitator	Each participant shall show a completed sticky note.	Black markers and sticky notes to write on	
09:30 AM	00:40	Dialogue on 4 questions	Joint dialogue on the 4 core questions. Participants submit responses on sticky notes, which are posted on the template (4 responses x 10 minutes).	Facilitator	If any additional input comes up along the way, this should be added on new sticky notes.	Extra sticky notes	
10:10 AM	00:20	Selection	Structuring, joint selection, and synthesis of the most relevant answers	Facilitator	Remove the sticky notes that were not selected.	Template, markers, and sticky notes	
10:30 AM	00:20	Collection and drawing	The group draws the final answers directly on the template.	Facilitator	Make sure writing is legible.	Template and markers	
10:50 AM	00:10	Conclusion and next steps	Recap. Thank you for participating. Member of the Executive Board talks about the next steps.	Executive members/ Facilitator	Clearly describe what the next steps entail.	Complete the template	
AFTER							
	00:10	Documentation, sharing, and clearing up	Take photo of completed template and share with participants. Template is rolled up and taken to the next step.	Facilitator			
	00:60	Processing of input	Facilitator and 2 members of the Executive Board meet to incorporate the participants' input in the strategy and prepare for distribution within the entire organization.	Executive members			

Playbook Designer

Work through situation, results, storyboard, and schedule; draw it up on sticky notes, paper, and whiteboard; or download and complete this tool. Take photos of your work and place everything into a manageable document that you can easily share.

HOW?

Work with the fields in the tool in the sequence that suits you best.

STICKY NOTES AND PAPER

Draw directly on the paper when you need to visualize the situation and results. Use sticky notes or paper for each step in your storyboard, so you can move steps around and test their sequence.

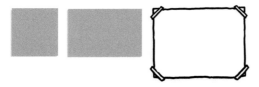

SCHEDULE

Download the Playbook Designer and Schedule on www.visualcollaboration.site.

PLAYBOOK FOR:_____

DATE:_____

BY:_____

SITUATION

TIME

PARTICIPANTS
ROLES/RESPONSIBILITIES/TASKS

PLACE

SETUP & EQUIPMENT

MATERIALS

SKETCH

RESULTS

STORYBOARD

BEFORE

DURING

AFTER

Summary

Scaling: A good playbook is particularly relevant when a process needs to be scaled. A good playbook gives you freedom and flexibility, ownership, and space for improvisation.

Design your playbook by
- Outlining the situation

- Visualizing anticipated results

- Creating a storyboard

- Creating a schedule

Playbook Designer: Use the Playbook Designer for structured work with the content of your playbook.

FOR WHAT PROCESS WOULD YOU
AND YOUR COLLEAGUES LIKE
TO MAKE A VISUAL PLAYBOOK?

6.
Enable Group Learning

ENABLE GROUP LEARNING

PURPOSE: TO PROVIDE YOU WITH A THEORETICAL
PERSPECTIVE ON VISUAL COLLABORATION

MANAGING COMPLEXITY
PAGE 206

SYSTEMS THEORY FOUNDATION
PAGE 208

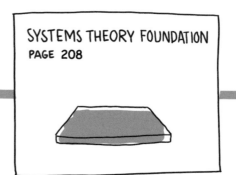

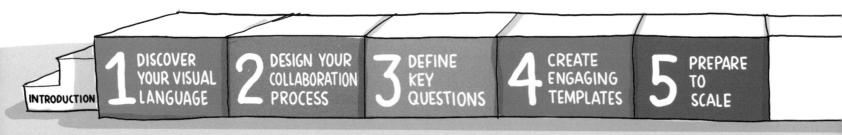

INTRODUCTION

1 DISCOVER YOUR VISUAL LANGUAGE

2 DESIGN YOUR COLLABORATION PROCESS

3 DEFINE KEY QUESTIONS

4 CREATE ENGAGING TEMPLATES

5 PREPARE TO SCALE

THE FIVE BUILDING BLOCKS

CHAPTER 6

GOAL: YOUR VISUAL COLLABORATION IS ROOTED IN A COHESIVE THEORETICAL FRAMEWORK

GROUP LEARNING
PAGE 218

THE VISUAL LEARNING ARENA
PAGE 220

6 ENABLE GROUP LEARNING

7 MAP YOUR SKILLS

8 ACTIVATE YOUR RESOURCES

9 DO'S & DON'TS

Managing complexity

You have now been through five chapters about a method that describes in practical terms how you can become more visual in your work. This chapter offers a theoretical perspective on the five practical chapters. It explains why we, as the principals of Bigger Picture in Denmark, do what we do and can guide you toward a more visual way of working, regardless of whether you do it on a large or small scale. We call our approach to working visually *system visualization*.

When we work visually, alone or together with others, we represent the world as we see it in images and words. We build up material that can be observed and interpreted. When we work with visualization in social processes, we approach this process with special attention to parts, relationships, and the way everything fits together. System visualization is a way of processing complexity so it becomes manageable.

System visualization is based on a set of fundamental *systems theory assumptions*, a focus on *group learning* and the idea that places where social processes unfold can be considered *visual learning arenas*.

Most professional processes we are part of are about understanding and expressing development, challenges, opportunities, or changes. But the world's complexity and the accelerating pace of change make it nearly impossible to grasp the entirety of anything. Decisions need to be made in the context of the bigger picture. In this chapter we will therefore introduce a few concepts that guide our work with people and organizations and that help us understand and operate within complex organizations and systems.

System visualization is a way of processing complexity so it becomes manageable.

3. THE VISUAL LEARNING ARENA

We design our physical environment so it stimulates the group's learning, knowledge, and systems understanding. A visual learning arena is the totality of layouts, artifacts, and visual templates.

2. GROUP LEARNING

We introduce collectivity into the learning concept and focus on the group rather than the individual.

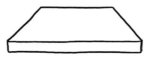

1. SYSTEMS THEORY FOUNDATION

A set of systems theory assumptions guide facilitators in facilitating processes and participants.

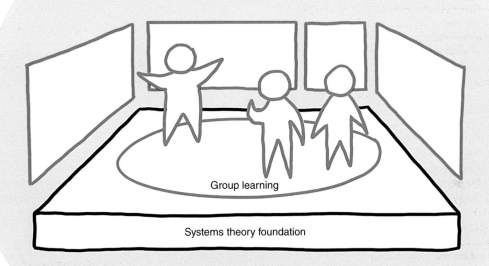

SYSTEM VISUALIZATION

Systems theory foundation

  SOCIAL SYSTEMS

Looking at the world from a systemic perspective rooted in the theories of Niklas Luhmann, social systems are at the core of our presence in the world.

Systems theory sees the person as a unit of a biological and psychic system. *Biological systems* create and maintain life. *Psychological systems* create and maintain consciousness. *Social systems* create and maintain communication.

All three types of systems produce and are constituted by the elements of which they consist—cells, thoughts, and communication, respectively. They are closed to one another in the sense that they do not understand one another, but they can utilize one another's resources nonetheless. The resources of the brain are neurons, which the psychological system employs in its creation of consciousness. The resources of the psychological system are thoughts, which influence the social system in the form of communicative inputs. The way in which people

come into contact with one another is through the third system, the social.

All people are in contact with a wide range of social systems throughout the course of their lives: family, school, friends, leisure clubs, teams of co-workers, or the workplace as a whole. Luhmann differentiates between three types of social systems: *interaction, organization,* and *society.*

Interaction: When we facilitate a process, we deal with people gathered in time and space and work with the social system. Organization: When we visualize an organization's strategy, working methods, or projects, we represent the organization's decision-making programs and work with a group through interaction, but based on the social system. We do not deal directly with the system society, as this system includes all communication that can be tied together and thus is infinitely complex.

THREE SYSTEMS

Biological
Creates and maintains life through cells

Psychological
Creates and maintains consciousness (thoughts, feelings, ideas)

Social
Creates and maintains communication

THREE TYPES OF SOCIAL SYSTEMS

Interaction
People assembled in time and space

Organization
Membership and decision-making programs

Society
Total amount of communication that can be connected

SOCIAL SYSTEMS

Management group

Organization

Interaction

Sales group

Employee group

Employee representation group

In a social systems process, you as a facilitator must relate to both the interaction you initiate and the social systems you activate. When, for example, we invite a group of organization members into a strategy dialogue, we are aware that these individuals do not communicate as a homogeneous group. A given manager represents a series of competences and personal characteristics that have bearing on the communication of the interaction, but he or she also represents a management system that communicates with defined structures of expectation for management. The same applies to an employee who, depending on function, can represent different systems in the organization.

An employee from the sales department establishes a communication perspective that focuses on sales/non-sales, but he or she may also be appointed as the employee representative and communicate in terms of employee satisfaction/non-satisfaction. To develop a common image of a strategy or to design a strategy dialogue, we need to do it so the interaction of the subsequent tool is meaningful across the various social systems of the organization.

System visualization is about making social systems the subject of our choices. We notice who and what is speaking when we represent communication visually. We need to be aware of what voices are not present in a process and which may be

over-represented. Well-designed processes with good visualizations are easy for process participants to fall in love with because decisions and visualizations in an interaction can appear nothing short of ideal. But they must resonate with colleagues who were not present to be effective beyond the meeting group.

Each of the five building blocks are designed with the social systems activated in a process in mind. For example, the ten process questions and associated tools in building block 2 are designed to ensure that an upcoming process is targeted to the social system or systems that need to interact.

COMMUNICATION

Social systems consist of communication. They arise and function by connecting communication with communication.

When you sit in on a meeting, for example, and a participant is speaking, and another follows, the interaction of the social system is underway, in the form of communication, which communicates in turn. Normally we say "I communicate" but in systems theory the "communication communicates." Communication can be observed on its own, separate from people, but naturally affected by the ideas and consciousnesses that launch it.

How does communication communicate? One thought follows another, which leads to a new one, which is influenced by something one sees, and which again leads to a new thought. This is also the way we can look at communication. Something is communicated, and the onward communication builds on the initial communication and forms the foundation of the

next communication. According to Luhmann, communication is therefore a chain reaction that is constantly moving forward by reaching back. Communication is thus a process that creates itself through itself.

This understanding of communication is made clear when working visually, because you are working in speech, text, and drawing, where text and drawing are anchored, so communication can easily move forward. And because it has been made visual, at the same time it clearly references what it reaches back into.

An important basic assumption in systems theory is that communication cannot be considered a straightforward and direct transfer of information from a sender to a receiver. Communication is, on the other hand, a three-part selection process that combines:
– Information
– Message
– Understanding

INFORMATION	MESSAGE FORM	UNDERSTANDING
Selection of message from many possible ones	Selection of message form	Selection of meaning from one's own viewpoint

A selection process takes place at each step of the communication. The message must be selected from among many possible messages. The message form must be chosen: Will the message be conveyed verbally? In an email or in a visual

representation? And finally, will the recipient understand the message as it was intended?

In systems theory, communication is not just about what is being communicated, but also how it is communicated, and how it is understood.

The term *process* is not understood as intended.

A visual language is a medium for communication and can help reduce possibilities of interpretation. Except for traditional symbols and icons that we encounter or find on our smartphones, a visual language is often not as influenced by routine interpretation as text and speech. Communication with visual artifacts delivers support and nuance. If we communicate in speech, text, and drawing alike, we gather meaning and expectations into terms that are available for further communication.

When, for example, we work with developing a visual language in building block 1, it is critical to be able to work in iterations so we can refine our way of understanding and using the terms and concepts in our work. A visual language is not static, but rather dynamic, and we need to be able to come back to terms and adjust them when new insights arise or when something changes.

The term *process* is understood as intended with the help of a visual artifact.

 AUTOPOIESIS

You may have tried to sit in on a meeting, as a guest in an organization, where everyone around the table speaks in codes, using expressions or half-phrases that are unintelligible, at least to you. If you are well-prepared, it's probably not your fault if you have a difficult time keeping up, but rather that the organization has simply become so self-referential that communication is no longer meaningful for outsiders.

Autopoiesis means "self-production or self-creation." The concept of autopoiesis makes it possible to observe social systems as independent and delimited and making only selective connections to their environment.

In the Question building block, there were a series of facilitation and visualization questions that can help you get a group to show what they mean by using visual artifacts. By defining and deciding how a group understands a concept, they select and delimit a given "something" over something else. When they do this visually, they are required to become specific, which often makes it easier for outsiders to understand.

In many organizations, a strategic plan is a good example of autopoiesis—a document that, while meticulously developed, may only be meaningful for a small exclusive circle.

It often refers to its environment through a matrix of customer relationships, competitors, or market trends, and it describes internal conditions, such as skills development or production development. But it is often a document that can prove difficult to decipher and process for an ordinary employee, because it was created within an insular management team.

The ordinary employee is, however, also part of subsystems in an organization such as a project unit. Here autopoiesis is also at play. The project unit defines itself by describing what falls inside the project responsibility and what falls outside it. The project unit therefore denotes itself in relation to its environment.

This selection and delimitation process is an important listening focus for any facilitator, because this continuous self-description often harbors internally understood meanings. Attribution of

meaning, when rendered visible and thus explicit, can help a system consciously shape or reshape itself through recognition of this self-image.

If, for example, you are working with the strategy template presented in this book, the various structured elements in the template will help the management team observe and clarify their strategy in a new way. It may still be difficult to decode for outsiders. The management team needs to be alert to what function the template is designed to serve, and for whom, and how intelligible it will be to those it needs to inform.

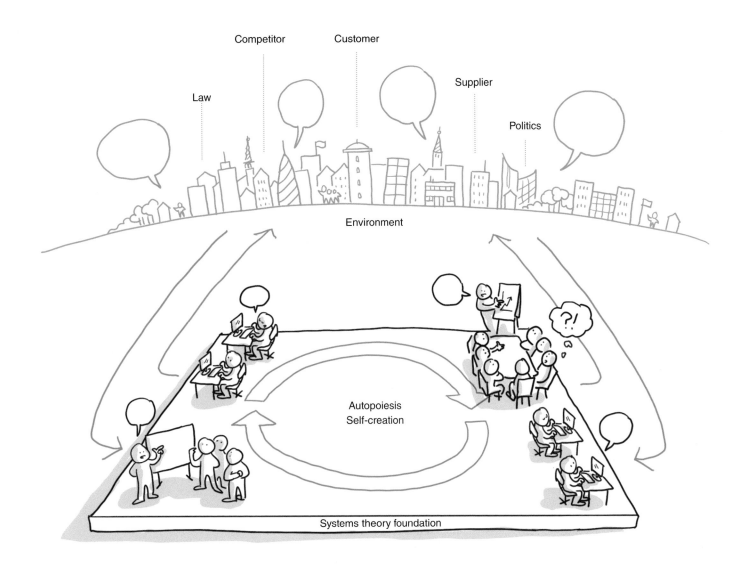

Model: A social system and autopoiesis

 **OBSERVATION**

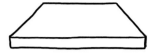

As a visual facilitator it is your role to help your participants see their process and to facilitate a corrective perspective when this proves necessary.

Our tireless focus on working with the purpose of a process is closely connected to our approach to regarding observation.

In formulating a purpose, we indicate what we are observing, and in the same sweep, what we are not observing.

Self-observation of social systems is essential for system visualization. Any organizational visual tool developed on the basis of system visualization has been developed through the self-observation of a system. If a project group develops a visual tool to support good meeting management, the tool will only create value when it is able to guide the group toward better meeting management through self-observation. The development of such a tool will only become possible when the group has defined how they observe and understand good meeting management.

Building block 2 is to a great extent developed to help a system observe.

By working with our observations we become aware of what it is we are excluding, and thereby become focused on what we are in fact observing.

This means that we define, very clearly and in visual terms, what falls within the framework of a given social process, while at the same time clarifying what falls outside the chosen framework and what we therefore will not incorporate into our work. Some of what falls outside our observation is not known to us; there are therefore blind spots inherent in our observation. There are things we know that we do not know, and things we do not know that we do not know.

In this sense, we are never working with "THE bigger picture" but always with "A bigger picture." Any group, organization, department, or project unit has a trove of high-potential images that can show wholes, but none that can show the whole.

The whole will always be observation-dependent, that is, dependent on how and when it is observed and by whom or what.

When a project group is to develop a visual tool to be able to function across their entire organization, they need to be able to notice both their own self-observation and their observation of the organization (environment). At the same time, the project group must understand that its observations are based on selections of inclusion and omission, and that these choices are formative to what emerges in the group's observations.

This approach reduces the risk that the tool will only be usable for the project group itself. A project group is a system in itself with its own attributions of meaning and its own logic. If it is to communicate successfully with others in the organization, the group must work consciously with its own autopoiesis, such as by looking at similarities and differences between itself and the organization.

Pen and paper are good tools that assist a group in seeing at every stage of a process. This can help your group understand through what lenses it is seeing itself.

Observation is not only about getting social systems to see something new, something else, or something more. It's about challenging them in their way of seeing and offering them new ways of seeing.

The project group creates a drawing showing others (outside the project group) using the yet-to-be developed meeting template. The project group works with these questions:
— Why do our colleagues need a meeting template?
— What do our colleagues say about the organization's meetings today?
— What do they say when they have held a meeting where they have used the new meeting template?

Systems theory foundation

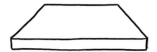

Core concepts of systems theory

SOCIAL SYSTEMS

Interactions, organizations, and societies are all social systems. They consist of communication that delineates itself from the environment by limiting further possibilities of communication.

COMMUNICATION

Communication is a process that creates itself through itself. Communication is a three-part selection process that combines information, message and understanding.

AUTOPOIESIS

Every system creates itself through itself and is only affected by its environment based on its own selections for inclusion and omission.

OBSERVATION

An observation is always a delimitation. Something is selected for inclusion, and something is selected for omission. An observation always has an observer who defines how something can be observed.

Visual collaboration

– Can strengthen social systems in self-preservation
– Can assist social systems in observing
– Can assist social systems in learning

– Can nuance communication by working in speech, text, and drawing
– Can anchor communication
– Can make communication observable

– Can clarify closure and self-reference
– Can overcome barriers to communication

– Is an observation tool
– Can help a group navigate its own observations

Group learning

Working on the basis of systems theory we can understand learning as a collective process rather than an individual one by focusing on the group and what it communicates.

Knowledge is valuable when it is applicable. Knowledge and experience do not necessarily guarantee survival in a changing world. The ability to continuously increase one's own knowledge and bring new knowledge into use does. This applies to individuals, groups, and organizations alike.

On the basis of systems theory we can look at a group's learning as something other than individual learning.

As an educator, facilitator, or manager we can choose, as shown in the figure to the right, to be attentive to the learning of each individual participant or to the learning of the group— in other words, to what is being communicated in the system.

The group's learning is always dependent on its own complexity and on the complexity of that section of the surrounding world that constitutes the group's whole. The group's learning requires a combination of knowledge that is maintained, and knowledge that changes through the group's connection to the environment.

The learning of social systems can therefore be described as an autopoetic process in which the social system itself, through communication, actively constructs knowledge on the basis of the group's connection to the environment. The approach to learning in this construction is deflected away from the individual.

Learning here is a collective autopoetic process where complexity is constantly increasing through communication. It is therefore important to work with the organization of communication in order to support and manage increasing complexity. We can approach this by verbally defining themes, hierarchies, and relationships.

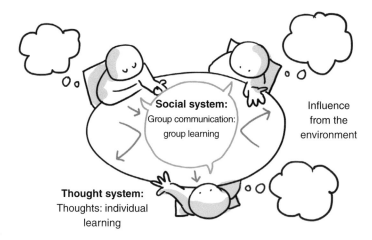

Social system:
Group communication:
group learning

Influence from the environment

Thought system:
Thoughts: individual learning

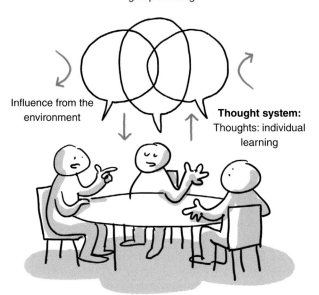

Social system:
Group communication:
group learning

Influence from the
environment

Thought system:
Thoughts: individual
learning

GROUP LEARNING

Focus is shifted from individual to group and centered
around what is being communicated. Group learning
requires a combination of knowledge that is maintained
and knowledge that changes through the group's connection to the environment.

LINGUISTICALLY ORGANIZED COMMUNICATION

In order to handle the increase in complexity in a learning group, themes are established hierarchies that are
defined and placed in relation to one another.

For example, when three themes are discussed in a
strategy meeting:

- What characterizes where we are today? (A)
- Where do we want to be in the future? (B)
- What challenges are we facing? (C)

The visual learning arena

A visual learning arena is the sum of visual templates, layouts, and elements that support group learning, knowledge, and system understanding.

The third and final layer of system visualization is the addition of visuals. A visual learning arena, in the simplest terms, is a flat surface you can write or draw on, such as a sheet of paper, a tablet, a whiteboard, or a flip chart. If you take personal notes for a meeting, in principle one could say that you are creating your own learning arena to support your thinking. But since we are focusing on collective learning, we will here pay attention to what we call the co-created visual learning arena. A visual learning arena is observable visual material, available for further communication, that ensures that knowledge can be maintained and changed. An active visual learning arena shows knowledge that needs to be arranged by theme hierarchy and placed in relationship through visual structures, models, symbols, and icons. It is jointly co-created through communication in text, speech, and drawing.

As you saw in building block 4, your learning arena can include an agenda, an overview of your project, and a template to collect new input. Each of these three templates thematizes a certain part of your communication and thus helps you manage your content and navigate it in both physical and mental terms.

A visual learning arena is a way of stimulating and supporting a group's learning. Your learning arena can contain multiple templates that each serve your purposes in their own way. If you and your colleagues are running projects that extend over longer periods of time, a good learning arena can allow you to move in and out of your process and pick up quickly where you left off. Structured work with a learning arena is also an effective means of inviting new participants into a process. They can quickly see where you have been and where you are, and thus get a better sense of where and how they can contribute going forward.

COMMUNICATION IN TEXT, SPEECH, AND DRAWING

By communicating in speech, text, and drawing, we reduce the chances of misinterpretation among recipients. We capture meaning and expectations in concepts that are available for further communication.

HANDLING INCREASED COMPLEXITY

Structured management of communication in text and drawings ensures organic control of a group's increasing complexity. A visual learning arena stimulates and supports group learning.

The visual learning arena in practice

BEFORE

The physical space is prepared to accommodate the hanging of paper for drawing or previous communication in the form of models, presentations, and the like. A whiteboard and projector are prepared.

DURING

The participants communicate in speech, text, and drawing. Key points are summarized and the communication is jointly synthesized. Each participant influences, shapes, and reshapes the communication in interaction with the others. The participants move around in a visual representation of individual and group learning.

AFTER

The process owner is responsible for closing the learning arena and for ensuring that the anchored communication is easy to understand when revisited by the group or fine-tuned and sent onward to the outside world, a new system, or another department, team, or organization.

Summary

System visualization is a way of conceptualizing and working with social processes in which visual collaboration is played out. System visualization is a particular approach to working visually.

Complexity management: System visualization is a way of processing complexity so it becomes manageable.

Systems theory foundation: With a foundation in systems theory, we work with four core concepts—social systems, communication, autopoiesis, and observation.

Group learning: We focus on group learning rather than individual learning. With the systems theory in hand we can work with linguistic organization of communication.

The visual learning arena: We support and stimulate group learning through our learning arenas and can thereby manage a greater level of complexity.

WHAT WOULD YOU LIKE TO CREATE
A VISUAL LEARNING ARENA FOR?

7.
Map your skills

MAP YOUR SKILLS

PURPOSE: TO INTRODUCE YOU TO EIGHT CORE SKILLS OF VISUAL COLLABORATION

THREE COMPETENCE AREAS

PAGE 230

EIGHT SKILLS

PAGE 232

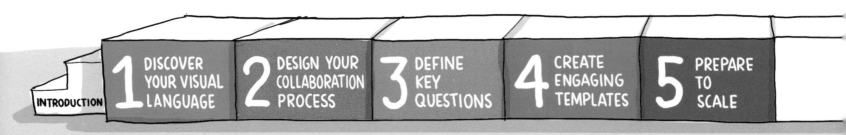

INTRODUCTION

1 DISCOVER YOUR VISUAL LANGUAGE

2 DESIGN YOUR COLLABORATION PROCESS

3 DEFINE KEY QUESTIONS

4 CREATE ENGAGING TEMPLATES

5 PREPARE TO SCALE

THE FIVE BUILDING BLOCKS

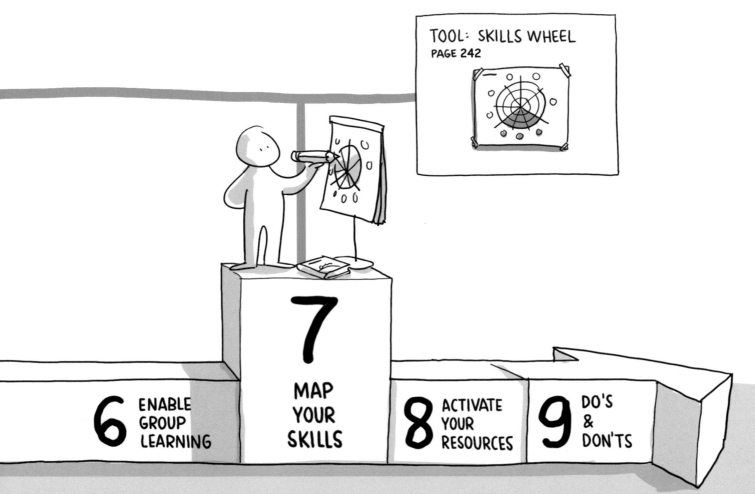

CHAPTER 7

GOAL: YOU KNOW THE SKILLS OF VISUAL COLLABORATION AND HOW TO CULTIVATE THEM

TOOL: SKILLS WHEEL
PAGE 242

6 ENABLE GROUP LEARNING

7 MAP YOUR SKILLS

8 ACTIVATE YOUR RESOURCES

9 DO'S & DON'TS

Three competence areas

We have identified three competence areas that we find particularly useful to master when you are facilitating, preparing, or otherwise working visually.

SYSTEM COMPETENCE

The ability to advance system understanding; creating and showing contexts and wholes.

FACILITATION COMPETENCE

The ability to sense a group and help it find its way forward.

VISUALIZATION COMPETENCE

The ability to handle and develop visual and written material that creates resonance.

Eight skills

Under each of the three competence areas, we have selected a series of practical skills to practice if you wish to improve at working visually.

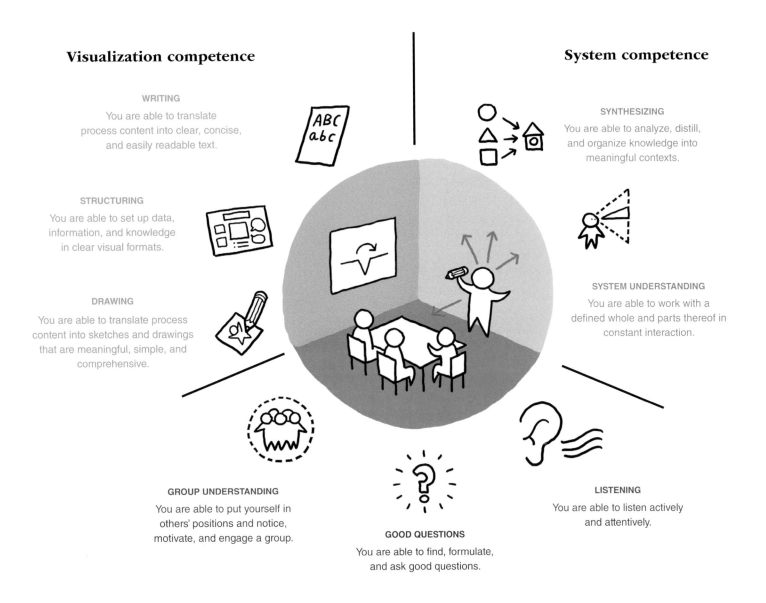

Visualization competence

WRITING
You are able to translate process content into clear, concise, and easily readable text.

STRUCTURING
You are able to set up data, information, and knowledge in clear visual formats.

DRAWING
You are able to translate process content into sketches and drawings that are meaningful, simple, and comprehensive.

System competence

SYNTHESIZING
You are able to analyze, distill, and organize knowledge into meaningful contexts.

SYSTEM UNDERSTANDING
You are able to work with a defined whole and parts thereof in constant interaction.

GROUP UNDERSTANDING
You are able to put yourself in others' positions and notice, motivate, and engage a group.

GOOD QUESTIONS
You are able to find, formulate, and ask good questions.

LISTENING
You are able to listen actively and attentively.

Facilitation competence

Group understanding

To see from other people's perspectives, sense a group, and motivate and engage it.

WHY?

Group dynamics are important; they have an impact on what a group can achieve. A group's ability to collaborate and learn together is advanced when the individual group participant feel that they are part of a community. This happens when each person is seen, heard, and understood. If you can facilitate this, you are creating both a good foundation for your shared work and legitimacy around your role as a facilitator. If you can at the same time show that you understand the needs of the group and work with them in a structured way, this will be reflected in your visual learning arena and create resonance with your participants.

IN PRACTICE

– You are well-prepared and have a solid sense of who your participants are and what they consider important.

– You see the individual and the group in a balanced interaction.

– You do not let the needs of a single participant overshadow the needs of the group.

– You can sense if a group is dysfunctional and act accordingly.

Good questions

To find, formulate, and ask good questions.

Good questions advance dialogue and innovation. As a facilitator it is important to be good at formulating good questions in advance and on the spot plus know how and when to tune into and ask for other questions the participants may have. Questions create the framework for what to talk about and visualize in a given process. Some questions are open and encourage exploration and investigation into new knowledge. Closing questions drive decision, and conclusions. Your questions are what determines the quality of the dialogue that is created, and thereby also the content that is visualized. Allowing a poor question can derail a process, exclude someone from a dialogue, or damage your legitimacy as a facilitator. It is an extremely valuable skill to be good at analyzing a series of questions and making sure that all the questions are well-constructed and asked in a productive sequence, and to discern the right questions to ask as the process unfolds.

IN PRACTICE

- You can design, formulate, and structure good questions.

- You know what questions can get everyone on track regarding a given topic.

- You ask for and include the questions of the participants.

- You are attentive to the construction of a question.

- You know when a question opens a dialogue and when it closes a dialogue.

- You see when a question is not appropriate.

- You use questions to guide a group to listen to one another, change perspective, and reach their own conclusions and usable results.

- You have a series of questions that you know work in various situations and you have experience in using them actively.

- You know which questions work best in speech and which work best as text in a template.

235

Listening

To listen actively and attentively.

WHY?

When you actively listen to your participants, you get an understanding of them both as individuals and as a group. You can then ask questions that are relevant specifically for them. When you listen actively, you show your participants recognition and respect, and this is important when you wish to have their engagement and input in the process. Listening to the participants, you gain greater knowledge and understanding of what they are meeting to discuss. This is what creates valuable visual results.

IN PRACTICE

– You are well-prepared and know what to listen for, because you know the context, purpose, and goal of the process.

– You are attentive to people: who is speaking, what they are saying, what words they emphasize, and how they use body language.

– You put your own inner critic and advisor on hold and just listen with an open mind.

– You indicate with your body language, gestures, and small verbal affirmations (yes, OK, aha) that you are focusing your attention on the person who is speaking.

– You occasionally repeat what you have heard and get your participants to nod to ensure that you have understood what is being said.

Writing

To translate process content into clear, concise, and easily readable text.

WHY?

When working visually it is important that others are able to read and understand what you write, including the material you have created in advance, what you create along the way, and what you produce after a process. Well-formulated and legible writing is essential for knowledge sharing and engagement.

IN PRACTICE

- You are well-prepared and use your writing skills to prepare your learning arena before the process starts, so your participants feel expected and welcome.

- You can reduce long sentences into shorter ones but preserve their essence.

- Writing is a significant part of your facilitation. All relevant content of the process is compiled into words and phrases.

- You show that you listen and understand by compiling input from your participants into text.

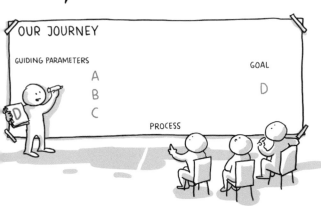

Drawing

To translate process content into sketches and drawings that are meaningful, simple, and comprehensive.

WHY?

Drawing is a tool for communication. It is a tool that supports understanding and dialogue. When you draw something you are thinking, a clarification process takes place. Some things work on paper and others do not. This visual selection allows opportunity for reflection for both you and your participants. Quick, unfinished sketches invite your participants to think further and draw with you. When we draw and sketch in a process, we experiment, explore, and clarify a subject together with our participants.

IN PRACTICE

- Before a process you produce visual templates that frame what you are meeting to discuss.

- Along the way you draw small illustrations showing details and large visual concepts, giving a sense of shared understanding and unity.

- You work with sketches and are not afraid of making mistakes.

- Before, during, or after a process you create a visual language that is tailored to the topic of the process.

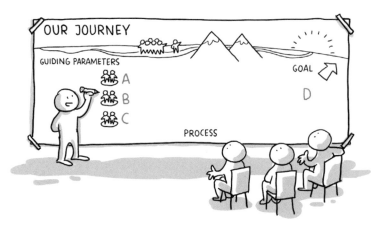

Structuring

To set up data, information and knowledge in clear visual formats.

WHY?

A good layout helps the eye navigate through visual material as easily as possible. It has to be easy to see what belongs together, what sequence things occur in, and what hierarchies and relationships various elements have in relation to one another. A good layout indicates a clear direction of reading and supports the "reader" in using the visual tool correctly.

IN PRACTICE

– You prepare templates and playbooks so they are easy to use for your participants.

– You plan the shape, size, and use of colors so it is easy to see patterns and contexts along the way in a process.

– You work with perspective to create calm for the eye and provide a sense of flow, movement, and time.

– You take your time during the process to make your visual material easy for the eye to navigate.

Synthesizing

To analyze, distill, and organize knowledge into meaningful contexts.

WHY?

Synthesis means "setting together"; *analysis* means "taking a whole apart and looking at the individual parts." The ability to analyze and see contexts and design and create an overview is essential in a complex world. It creates clarity for your participants when you are able to convert what is being discussed and to give it back to your participants in a coherent visual form that is easy to understand and possible to act on.

IN PRACTICE

– You listen and see what belongs together and what elements differ from one another.

– You hear the levels on which the discussion unfolds, what topics are addressed, and what ties things together.

– You conclude a dialogue by summarizing the key points of what has been said.

– You gather fragments into wholes so they becomes meaningful for your participants.

System understanding

To work with the whole and parts of the whole in constant interaction.

System understanding, at its core, is relevant for anyone operating in social interaction. With a systems theory foundation we have a basic assumption that there are many world views and truths, and that nobody can grasp the world objectively. Working on the basis of this perspective helps you and your participants understand and manage complexity.

IN PRACTICE

- You make preparations before a process to know who your participants are and what content you will be working with.

- You allocate time and employ questions that invite your participants to work with multiple perspectives.

- You often take a step back and get a sense of how what you are working on fits into the bigger picture of a given context. You invite participants to do the same.

- You stimulate the overview of your participants by offering visual concepts that contain a given whole.

- You ask questions that create awareness of potential blind spots.

- You work with versions and acknowledge that nothing is finished or final.

Skills Wheel

Use the Skills Wheel to map your profile and get an overview of what skills it would benefit you to practice. Evaluate on a scale from 1 to 5 the degree to which you currently master each skill.

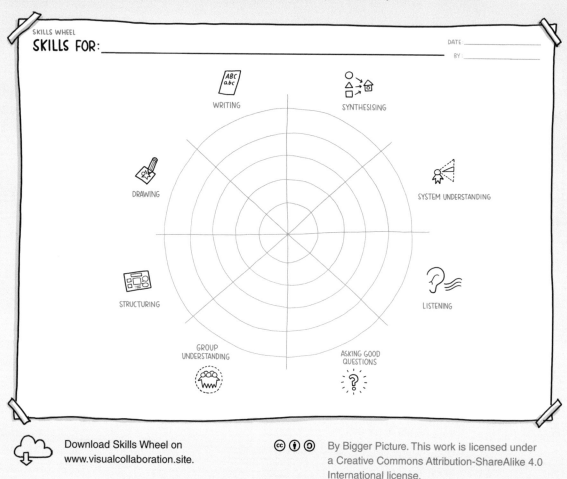

SKILLS WHEEL

SKILLS FOR: _____   DATE _____

                                                      BY : _____

- WRITING
- SYNTHESISING
- DRAWING
- SYSTEM UNDERSTANDING
- STRUCTURING
- LISTENING
- GROUP UNDERSTANDING
- ASKING GOOD QUESTIONS

PROFILES

The Skills Wheel can be completed individually or collectively. Expand the wheel with the skill or skills that are missing in relation to your individual or collective needs.

Examples

Strong visual practitioner who is not trained in facilitation or enabling of system understanding.

Strong facilitator who feels at home in most processes but who does not yet have a mastery of the more visual skills.

Beginner who has tried everything but does not yet feel secure in any of the selected skills.

Summary

Three competence areas to master when you want to work more visually:

1. Facilitation competence

2. Visualization competence

3. System competence

Eight skills to practice if you wish to get better at working more visually:

– Group understanding

– Good questions

– Listen

– Write

– Draw

– Structure

– Synthesis

– System understanding

Skills Wheel: You can use the Skills Wheel to map your individual or team profile.

WHAT SKILLS DO YOU NEED
TO IMPROVE THE MOST?

8.
Activate your resources

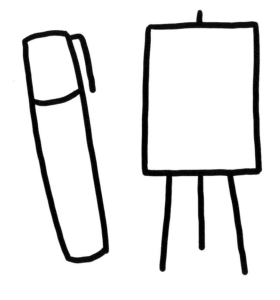

ACTIVATE YOUR RESOURCES

PURPOSE: TO INTRODUCE YOU TO THE MOST IMPORTANT RESOURCES OF VISUAL COLLABORATION

PARTICIPANTS
PAGE 252

FACILITIES
PAGE 254

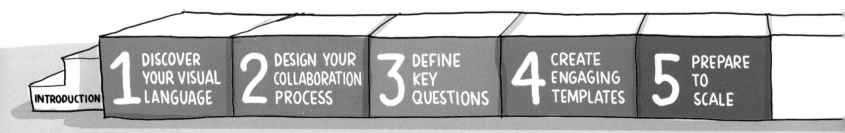

INTRODUCTION

1 DISCOVER YOUR VISUAL LANGUAGE

2 DESIGN YOUR COLLABORATION PROCESS

3 DEFINE KEY QUESTIONS

4 CREATE ENGAGING TEMPLATES

5 PREPARE TO SCALE

THE FIVE BUILDING BLOCKS

CHAPTER 8

GOAL: YOU KNOW HOW BEST TO ACTIVATE YOUR RESOURCES

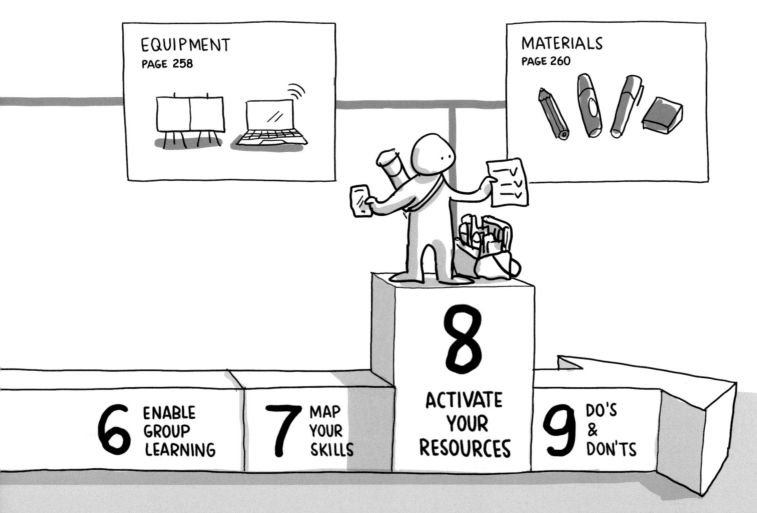

EQUIPMENT
PAGE 258

MATERIALS
PAGE 260

6 ENABLE GROUP LEARNING

7 MAP YOUR SKILLS

8 ACTIVATE YOUR RESOURCES

9 DO'S & DON'TS

Choice of resources

All meetings, projects, and processes are different and place different requirements on your resources. Your participants are your most important resource—without them there is no process. All other resources, such as your facilities, equipment, and materials, must be used in a way that they best support the work and engagement of your participants and the purpose of the process.

Whether you need to facilitate a smaller dialogue or design a large-scale conference, it is important to consider how best to put the available resources into play. If, for example, you forget to take the acoustics of the facilities into consideration, even a well-planned process can fail because your participants can't hear anything.

Participants

Activate your main resource by giving roles and responsibilities to your participants so it becomes clear to everyone who does what before, during, and after a process. Here is an overview of the roles and responsibilities that it might be good to delegate or pay additional attention to when working visually in large-scale processes.

PROCESS OWNER

A process owner has a particular interest in achieving the goal of the process. A process owner has the authority to enact changes at all levels of the process. Close collaboration between process owner and process designer or visual facilitator is therefore necessary in order to ensure unity about the goal of the process and how it is achieved.

HOST

A host makes the facilities available where the process takes place. Build your learning arena in close collaboration with your host.

PARTICIPANT

The participants may have many different roles and responsibilities along the way in a process, for example, as passive listeners during a presentation and as active participants in group work, where the participant's knowledge is used in interaction with that of others. Consider how best to bring the resources of your participants into play in ways that promote the best possible results.

PRESENTER

A presenter has knowledge that is relevant for both the participants of the process and the purpose of the process. A presenter is responsible for presenting knowledge that is understandable and usable for the participants.

GROUP HOST

A group host is responsible for supporting the process and results in group work. Appoint a group host when you are operating with large groups that must co-create a result or when your subject or design has a high level of complexity.

VISUAL FACILITATOR

A visual facilitator forms and supports communication and interaction in a group of people through guiding questions and system visualization.

PROCESS ILLUSTRATOR

A process illustrator collects the key points of the content of a process and builds visual structures and language to support the participants in seeing the content of the process along the way.

ASSISTANT

An assistant is always two steps ahead of a process with an overview of time, materials, catering, process documentation, and participant care.

TECHNICIAN

Make the technician your new best friend. It is nice to be able to shift between your analog and digital tools when you want. Know your technician's first name and contact details.

Facilities

Establish requirements for your facilities, because this is what forms the supporting framework of your learning arena. Your facilities must support your process by giving your participants adequate fresh air, good sound quality for discussions and presentations, and flexible space to work together.

OFFICE

If you wish to work visually as part of your everyday operations, make sure to arrange your environment to make it possible. Make it easy to hang paper on the wall, or move your desk around so you have a place to work in analog format.

MEETING FACILITIES

Space is particularly important when you are working visually, and it pays to be looking for that extra bit of space when booking meeting facilities for visual collaboration. Book a space that offers room for twice the number of participants as are actually attending, so there is space to see, develop, and draw together. Use the entire room, hang up context-relevant materials, post the meeting's program and purpose so everyone can see it, and make sure it is possible to move around in the space as the process moves forward.

Many organizations are not yet geared to work as visually as this book recommends. Think of easy, creative ways to free up space to work visually. In most cases you can make things work with a little rearrangement and then you will have the environment you need to work effectively with pen and paper.

WORKSHOP FACILITIES

Workshop facilities are often flexible in their layout. Take a little extra time to think of the right setup for your process. If you are going to be working in groups, it can be a good idea to screen off each group and create small learning spaces within the room. This strengthens the focus of group participants and at the same time gives the facilitator an overview of all the groups at once and the opportunity to deliver common messages along the way.

CONFERENCE FACILITIES

Conference facilities are often large and therefore most suitable for processes with more than 50 participants. Like workshop facilities, they are flexible in their layout. Size has advantages and disadvantages. Having a lot of space is good, but processes can also be drowned out by poor acoustics and too many people. Make sure there is appropriate technical equipment so everyone can hear what is being said. Large visual events require planning down to the smallest detail. It is a discipline in itself to manage group work involving 80 participants. Position the group tables close together and create a natural center of gravity toward the podium.

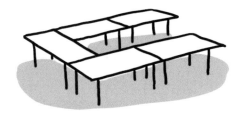

Table layout

The way we sit in a space influences our behavior. What table layout suits your process best? Table layouts can both support an organizational hierarchy and neutralize it.

MEETING TABLES

A classic layout with a table in the middle and chairs around it helps ensure that all the participants in the meeting can hear one another and see a common projector, screen, or whiteboard.

U-SHAPED TABLES

A formation where the participants sit alongside one another facing the middle of the room is well-suited to presentations or meetings where there is one speaker at a time.

Atmosphere

The right amount of light, sound, and air has an impact on your participants' ability to concentrate. The same applies to catering and the number of breaks.

LIGHTING

If the participants are to be able to see what they are drawing and present it to one another, it is important for there to be good lighting in the facilities. Make sure to bring additional light sources.

SOUND

Always try to get facilities with good acoustics, so the participants can easily hear what is being said. It is also good to arrange one's process so as to shift between periods of quiet, dialogue, open conversation, and music.

GROUP TABLES

Group tables direct the focus of group work. Here the participants have a good opportunity to delve into group work while still remaining part of the larger whole.

TABLES IN ROWS

If your participants are sitting at tables in long rows facing one end of the facilities, you are setting things up for one-way communication. Group work can, however, function on a small basis with two to three participants.

CHAIRS ONLY

If there are only chairs available in your facilities, and you are planning for your participants to work visually, equip each participant with a clipboard, as this allows for visual reflection between neighbors.

AIR

A space where there is not enough oxygen can drain all the energy and concentration out of the participants. It is also difficult to work effectively if the facilities are too cold or too hot. Keep an eye on temperature and air circulation.

FOOD

Our brains need nourishment. A full day of concentration and focus demands extra nutrition. Providing water, fruit, tea, coffee, and healthy snacks for the sharp minds of participants before the need arises creates a relaxed atmosphere.

BREAKS

It's useful to take breaks at the right times and before the participants lose concentration. Take breaks when changing between forms of work and to create space for reflection or rest. Break the process up so it feels dynamic.

Equipment

If you want to work more visually, don't skimp on equipment. Here is an overview of equipment you should generally have on hand and equipment that can be good to have for large-scale processes with many participants or when working in global teams.

Analog equipment

WHITEBOARD

A whiteboard is a flexible tool for sketching. It is a fundamental resource if you work visually on a regular basis. Whiteboards are available in a wide range of formats and sizes, from very small (less than an 8½" × 11" sheet) to very large. Use paint to make any surface into a usable whiteboard; whiteboards of sustainable materials are also available.

MOBILE WALLS

Mobile walls may be necessary if there is not enough wall space in your facilities. These can also be used for screening during group work or can be taken out into the open. Having mobile walls ensures that you do not need to let operations be dictated by the facilities you find along the way. With mobile walls you can always build the learning arena that best suits your process.

FLIP CHART

Flip charts are a good tool for smaller group work processes or short meetings. They are easy to move around and also easy to come by in most organizations.

Digital equipment

TABLET

If you are working with visual communication every day a tablet is a vital tool. It can be used to pre-design templates, gather processes, and draw live together with others. There are many different tablets available, with a great range in price and features. Look for software that is simple enough that you don't need to learn a complicated drawing program before you can get started.

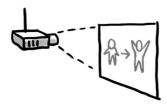

PROJECTOR

A projector is an effective tool when you need to share information with a large group of people. Use a projector when you want to present your templates for group work, go through the day's visual agenda, or show complex images of the whole, slide by slide.

CAMERA

Most people now have a highly functional camera in their mobile phone. Use it to document your process. Remember, in particular, to take pictures of completed group templates and other completed materials. If you conduct many processes or do a lot of whiteboard sketches, a camera that takes high-resolution images can be a good investment.

LARGE MULTITOUCH SCREENS

Large digital whiteboards make it possible for several people to draw, write, and organize information together without having to be in the same office or, for that matter in the same country. These screens are still expensive, and using them requires training. But when they work, they are—and will become even more—effective for both analog and virtual meetings where they can save time, CO_2, and the cost of airfare.

Materials

Good quality, fresh materials give you freedom to focus on what is important. Try out different materials and use the ones that suit you best.

FINE BLACK MARKERS

Used to write and draw on smaller formats such as in personal reflection tools, in notebooks, or on sticky notes. Use them instead of a ballpoint pen, which might be difficult to see at a distance and in photos.

MEDIUM BLACK MARKERS

Used for text and drawings on flip charts and templates. Help your participants work with key points when they write densely without leaving space for long, meticulous phrases.

GRAY BRUSH MARKERS

Used to create simple shadows and create depth and perspective in both text and drawings.

BOLD COLOR MARKERS

Colors allow you to color-code. Use them when you are facilitating, place them on group tables during group work, and instruct your participants in working with color coding.

WHITEBOARD MARKERS

Get your own set of whiteboard markers and always have them with you. They come in a wide range of colors and are essential for visual collaboration.

COLORED CHALK

With chalk you can quickly color in large areas, adding life and depth.

STICKY NOTES

These small self-adhesive papers are available in many colors and formats—make balanced use of them. Design your templates so they fit the sticky notes you will be using. Use them in group work when everyone needs to be on track. Use their colors strategically when you are grouping topics. Use their flexibility to reorganize, prioritize, discard, and add new.

ROLL PAPER

A large roll of paper makes it possible to work in whatever sizes the walls of a given space allow. Measure, tear off, and set up—work in a wide format. A roll of paper is available from most suppliers in sizes 60-90 cm high.

TAPE

There are three kinds of tape that are always good to have on hand:
– Masking tape: This allows you to hang your templates and large pieces of paper on all kinds of surfaces.
– Cellophane tape: Good to have on hand to repair posters or arrange piece of information in new ways.
– Correction tape: There is a great freedom in being able to make corrections and deletions in what you are doing. With correction tape you can stick white strips of paper over mistakes or changes.

NOTEPAD

Notepads are good for quick sketches, and gathering information and ideas that need to be remembered. Use pads with blank pages so you are not limited by lines or grids. In processes over a longer period of time, it can be valuable to distribute notepads to all your participants.

SCISSORS/KNIVES

Rolls of paper need to be cut, and content from one context can be cut out and merged into another. Scissors and knives make possible new formats, combinations, and collages.

Summary

Participants: Activate your participants so they assume responsibility, take ownership, and engage in the process.

Facilities: Establish requirements for your facilities, as this is what forms the supporting framework of your learning arena. Sometimes all it takes are a few simple changes at no cost to make your process a success.

Equipment: Don't skimp on equipment. Visual collaboration requires good analog and digital equipment and tools.

Materials: Make yourself a good toolbox and always have it with you.

WHAT WOULD IT TAKE
TO MAKE YOUR ORGANIZATION
READY FOR A MORE VISUAL
WAY OF WORKING?

9.
Do's and dont's

DO'S & DON'TS

PURPOSE: TO HIGHLIGHT STRENGTHS AND WEAKNESSES OF VISUAL COLLABORATION

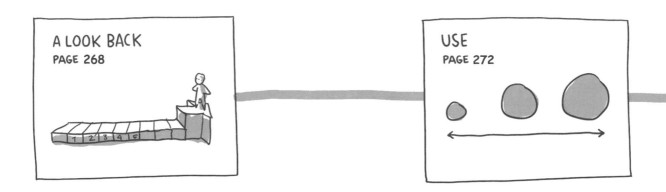

A LOOK BACK
PAGE 268

USE
PAGE 272

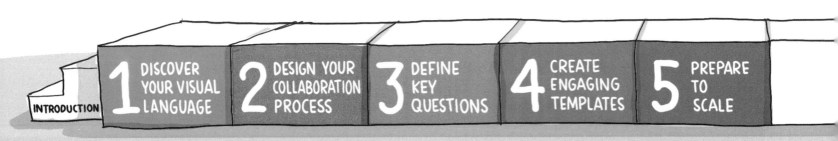

INTRODUCTION

1 DISCOVER YOUR VISUAL LANGUAGE

2 DESIGN YOUR COLLABORATION PROCESS

3 DEFINE KEY QUESTIONS

4 CREATE ENGAGING TEMPLATES

5 PREPARE TO SCALE

THE FIVE BUILDING BLOCKS

CHAPTER 9

GOAL: YOU ARE ALL SET FOR SUCCESSFUL VISUAL COLLABORATION

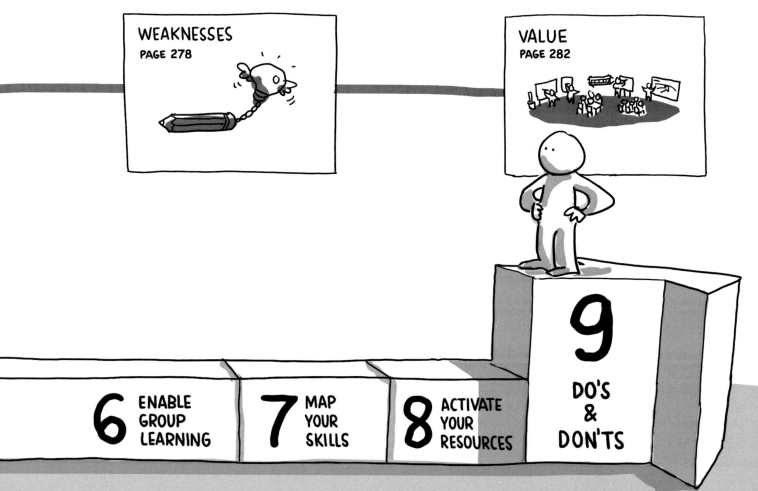

WEAKNESSES
PAGE 278

VALUE
PAGE 282

6 ENABLE GROUP LEARNING

7 MAP YOUR SKILLS

8 ACTIVATE YOUR RESOURCES

9 DO'S & DON'TS

A look back

With the Five Building Blocks of Visual Collaboration and system visualization, we hope you have gained new perspectives on how you can use visualization to achieve—and give others—better system understanding.

On the following pages you will find:

– An overview of the Five Building Blocks of Visual Collaboration
– Perspectives on visual collaboration: in large or small scale, with no time for planning, and getting your participants drawing together with you
– A list of some of the weaknesses that you may encounter when working visually
– Perspectives on the value visual collaboration can deliver

6 ENABLE GROUP LEARNING

7 MAP YOUR SKILLS

8 ACTIVATE YOUR RESOURCES

9 DO'S & DON'TS

The Five Building Blocks of Visual Collaboration™

BUILDING BLOCK	1. Discover your visual language	2. Design your collaboration process
METHOD	A method to develop a visual language for meetings, processes, and projects, regardless of content	A method to develop and visualize processes, regardless of content
WHAT	The Seven Elements™ and The Eighth Element™	Ten process questions
TOOLS	 Icon Designer	 Process Designer
OUTCOME	Visual artifacts to support communication	Cohesive visual process design

3. Define key questions	**4. Create engaging templates**	**5. Prepare to scale**
A method to formulate process-relevant facilitation and visualization questions	A method to develop templates for any meeting, project, or process	A method to develop visual playbooks
Design guide to categorize, prioritize, and test questions for a process design	Guide to design function, form, size, and structure of a template	Design guide to describe the situation and results of a process and create a storyboard and schedule

Question Designer

Template Designer

Playbook Designer

Prioritized facilitation and visualization questions	Templates to manage information and dialogue	Scalable process design

Use

Small and large scale

The Building Blocks are a method you can use in countless variations, depending on requirements.

A dialogue with a colleague about two good questions and an empty whiteboard is one way of using the method. Using visual tools in the planning of an event is another, even if you are not planning an event where pen and paper will be used.

The method is flexible, and it can be used on a small scale, but it can also be used in very large-scale processes where each part of the method is at play and together with the other parts serves to deploy the method as a whole.

Without planning

What happens when something changes and the process you have planned no longer makes sense? Or when a need arises now and there is no time for planning? Here are a few suggestions of how to navigate in spur-of-the-moment processes.

How do I do all this in the middle of a meeting when the need comes up? The simple answer is: Practice! To spontaneously set up a whiteboard and visually facilitate a dialogue takes practice.

Fortunately, visual work is rewarding because our memory enjoys visual material. We easily remember the drawings, sketches, visual languages, and templates that we create. They imprint themselves in our memory. We cannot always reuse the same old drawings or templates. But once you have a portfolio of four to eight templates that you have used in various processes, you will have built up valuable process experience and a strong visual library that your memory can revisit and seek inspiration from when you are suddenly in a meeting and the need arises.

You can combine icons from previous themes for which you have created visual language and in this way spontaneously develop icons for the given context.

You can recall visual structures from old templates and put them together in new ways so they form a new and usable framework for the current process.

Drawing ⟶

Denominator ⟶

Every time you prepare, you are creating a stronger base on which to act in the moment. You are extending the visual repertory that your memory can reach back into and use to create new icons and templates. Every time you create and use a process design with related questions and visual tools, it makes you better at taking responsibility for—and facilitating—a process spontaneously.

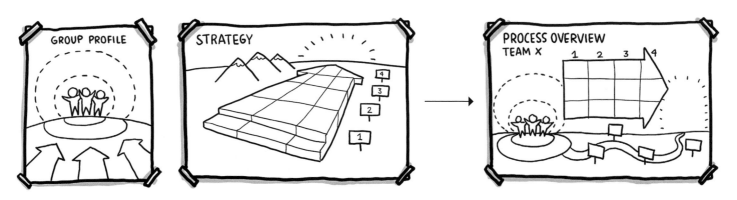

Involvement

Visual collaboration is new for many people. It can be useful to get your process participants on board with *why* and *how* you will be working visually before you begin.

INTRODUCTION

Always give your process participants a few good reasons for working visually. Show them how you will be working and why before you get them drawing. Some of our most commonly used reasons cited for the importance of visual collaboration are:

- It is easier to remember than speech or text alone.
- It engages and creates good energy.
- We literally "see what you mean."
- Visualization helps us see contexts and connections and build a "whole" we could not see without the benefit of others' perspectives.

EQUIPMENT

Make sure that all your participants have the right equipment. Good equipment supports a serious and professional approach to visual work. Invest in quality markers—both fine and bold—notepads, large paper, and sticky notes. Use digital equipment and tools where they bring extra value.

EXERCISES

It is usually only a few people who dive into drawing and sharing right from the start. It takes a little practice. Create small, simple exercises that everyone can practice and that support your participants in working visually:

- Invite your participants to create personal name tags with a little icon showing their function, role, or profile. Have them present them to one another.
- Invite your participants to share their latest drawing. Many people actually draw without thinking about it. A graph or a model on a whiteboard is a kind of drawing.

TRAINING

We are always eager to invite our participants to draw, sketch, and think in images on their own. Most people can benefit from a few tips and tricks to draw more easily and quickly. Take five to ten minutes to introduce the basic symbols, the Seven Elements, and a few icons that are particularly relevant to your process or context.

SERIOUS PLAY

Many people are familiar with Pictionary as a game they play for fun with family or friends. We play it seriously with colleagues and business partners. But it's hard to avoid having fun in the process. It creates energy, stimulates a taste for competition in most people, and trains us both in bridging the right and left hemispheres of the brain and in listening and association. We have played Pictionary with as many as 1,500 conference participants. Play and build a strong visual language with your participants that is relevant to your specific meeting.

LEAD THE WAY

Show the way by sketching freely without hesitation. Don't dwell on small mistakes or on sketches that may look a bit childish. As long as what you create is meaningful and relevant, it does not need to be polished. You can thereby model that it is OK to "make mistakes" in presenting visual material. And you establish a practice of having verbal input be visually supported.

Weaknesses

Implicit in our approach is acknowledgment of the fact that there is no one "right" way of observing or representing the world. Every observation has its "blind spots." Visual collaboration is no different. It also has its limitations.

Some dialogues, comments, or meetings do not benefit from being placed into systems and represented visually; it is important to be able to recognize these situations when they arise, because after an initiative gets underway it can be difficult to shift gears if you determine that a specific approach is not working.

Sometimes the complexity is too overwhelming to be captured visually. It can't always be worked into a sketch or an overview image, and thinking that it can will end in frustration or oversimplification.

Not everyone is equally happy with visual components. Some people find visual material straining, confusing, and disruptive.

On the following pages we describe some of the challenges and limitations of visual collaboration. We have divided them into three categories where each independently relates to:

– Product: *The visual product or the concrete drawing*
– System: *People, groups, and organizations*
– Process: *Execution of visual processes*

Our list can alert you to shortcomings to be aware of when navigating with pen and paper. Add to the list based on your own experience.

Product

DRAWINGS CAN FREEZE A PROCESS OR DIALOGUE

A drawing, icon, or visual product can work against intentions when employed in the wrong context, form, or timing. It can freeze a process or dialogue and hinder further innovation and exploration of a given subject.

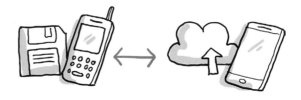

OUR VISUAL LANGUAGE OFTEN BUILDS ON THE PAST

Many of the icons we use today are grounded in outmoded ways of perceiving and thinking. Our language is full of worn-out metaphors, and technological development is much faster than our ability to change and adapt our communication accordingly. A visual language that points backward can anchor us in an outgrown past.

ANALOG TOOLS ARE UNWIELDY

Until we can all easily transfer analog tools such as posters, paper, and sticky notes seamlessly onto digital platforms, analog visual work has some drawbacks in time and physical organization required for setup and follow-up. Working visually sets demands for facilities and equipment and often requires time for setting up and dismantling a space, as well as a strategy for follow-up, digitization, and sharing.

BAD DRAWINGS ARE ALSO MEMORABLE

Our memory is geared toward remembering images and drawings; unfortunately, it doesn't separate out the bad ones. If a process, experience, or statement is captured visually in a form that creates negative or incorrect connotations, it requires effort to get participants to undo these connotations.

System

POLITICS AND RELIGION

Politics and religion are difficult to navigate and represent with pen and paper. Many people define themselves on the basis of political or religious affiliation, but it can be very sensitive to draw something about what we stand for, what we are, or what we believe in.

CULTURE

Humor, irony, and hierarchies are very different from culture to culture and from organization to organization. A drawing, color, or question can be understood entirely differently depending on where you are and whom you are talking to. The visual can be explosive in inter-cultural groups and can require additional caution.

FATIGUE

Many organizations experience a constant flow of new tools, processes, and methods to be implemented. Implementing a new visual working method in a tired organization can fail, especially in the absence of strong backing from management and the patience to wait for results.

THE BACK CAN'T LISTEN

When working visually, it is inevitable that you will sometimes have to turn your back to your participants when they are speaking in order to draw what is being said. But you can't listen with your back. This can be perceived as offensive and incite resistance from participants.

ALONE WITH PEN AND PAPER

It might be difficult to be the first one in your organization to start working visually. It often requires courage and resilience, because organizations, and organizational cultures in particular, are difficult to change. Convincing arguments, strong supporters, and patience are necessary.

YET ANOTHER DRAWING...

Like with everything else, the visual can become overwhelming. If we try to implement the visual in every single process, we can stop paying needed attention and stop using the method and tools as intended.

Process

IT'S TIME-CONSUMING

Working visually is time-consuming. It takes time to learn how to do, and it also takes time once you've gotten the hang of it.

THE VISUAL EXPOSES A PROCESS LACKING CONTENT

The content of a process becomes clear when it is visualized. But it also becomes clear when there is no content in a process, because then there is nothing to visualize. Poor presentations, group work that reaches a deadlock, or general discussions that turn in circles all result in painfully empty fields.

SPONTANEITY HAS LIMITS

Many visual tools are developed before a process, and it takes experience to change them along the way if the need arises. There is therefore a risk that spontaneity will be diminished by the existing frames, or a needed change in the process will be overlooked because each step is already planned out and has bearing on the next.

Value

Any organization can benefit from visual collaboration. The Five Building Blocks constitute a method that makes it easier to get started and can support and develop a more visual working culture.

Over the last 15 years we have trained more than 10,000 people in working visually. This includes teachers, presenters, meeting managers, students, politicians, consultants, change agents, managers, designers, and engineers.

We have developed more than 500 strategic tools large and small for a diverse range of organizations, and we have designed, facilitated, and drawn for a large number of meetings, workshops, and conferences.

It has been our experience that a visual working culture can strengthen the way people think, communicate, and collaborate.

It's not a quick fix, because it's a working method that requires both patience to learn and implement, and planning and backup to maintain.

The method can initially be learned by a few people and employed on a small scale so its effectiveness can be tested.

Here are some of the values we believe visual collaboration delivers.

EFFICIENCY AND CLARITY

When we work with system visualization, we can more easily invite others into our processes because they can see our purpose and goals. Visual tools make our decisions (or lack thereof) clear. When we work visually, we more quickly become aware of whether our communication is usable, guiding, and realistic to pursue.

STRONG KNOWLEDGE SYSTEMS

Visual learning arenas stimulate and support collective learning. By pooling knowledge into visual structures with context-relevant visual language, we advance system understanding and build strong knowledge systems that are not individual dependent. Visually mapped knowledge remains in an organization and is easy to share.

DIVERSITY AND INCLUSION

When linguistically navigating in a language other than our mother tongue, we are often slower, less nuanced, and more hesitant. System visualization is three-part communication, since you employ speech, text, and drawing. It facilitates communication even when taking place in a language other than our mother tongue, which is an advantage for any diverse organization.

ENGAGEMENT AND OWNERSHIP

System visualization promotes involvement and transparent decisions and expectations. It provides an overview and creates understanding, and these are the parameters that make our work more meaningful.

To sum up: Visual collaboration creates better results faster. And is more fun.

Summary

Application:

– Large scale and small: Start
small. All you need is an empty
whiteboard, a good question, and
a colleague to explore it with.

– Involvement: Involve your process
participants in why and how you
will be working visually.

– Without planning: Working visually
in spontaneous processes takes
practice, but the more processes
you design visually, the more
material your memory has to
reach back into and create
something new from.

Weaknesses:

Sometimes it's better just to put
down the pen.

Value:

Visual collaboration delivers:

– Efficiency and clarity

– Diversity and inclusion

– Strong knowledge systems

– Engagement and ownership

WHAT IS YOUR NEXT DRAWING?
HOW AND WHEN WILL YOU USE IT?

Appendix

The learning arena of this book

We invite you to use this physical setup for an upcoming meeting, project, or process. Download and print the tools or draw them. Work with the tools and experience how the panorama setup improves your overall content.

Inspiration

The following people, theories, and schools have served as inspiration for the different parts of the book.

Visualization and visual facilitation
Pioneer David Sibbet has been an important sparring partner since we first began our journey into visual facilitation. We have also found inspiring colleagues in the practice communities of the International Forum of Visual Practitioners, VizThink, and EuViz.

Process design, process consultation, and facilitation
Our approach to facilitation comes to a large extent from the Kaospilots, where our way of working with process design, in particular, was inspired by Dee Hock and his theory on the chaordic organization.

Question
Our work on questions was inspired by William Isaacs, Sam Kaner, Juanita Brown, and David Isaacs. We have also benefited from many conversations with Carsten Ohm and many informal master classes with Bliss Browne—two experts in the art of asking powerful questions.

Systems theory
Our systems theory foundation is based on the conceptual framework of Niklas Luhmann, but our understanding of Luhmann's concepts has been greatly assisted along the way by a number of Danish system theorists. We have been particularly inspired by Niels Åkerstrøm Andersen, Ole Thyssen, and Jens Rasmussen. Niels Åkerstøm Andersen gave us feedback on chapter 6. Jens Rasmussen provided critiques, advice, and guidance for the whole book.

Organizational learning
We have drawn inspiration from the two pioneers of organizational learning, Peter Senge and Otto Scharmer. Both have been involved with system thinking and system change, and each in their own way has worked with learning in large systems.

Credits

Citations, models, tools, and illustrations.

Chapter 1: Icon design
Page 44: David Sibbet introduced us to the star figure in 1996. We have been drawing and training others to draw people in this simple way ever since.

Chapter 2: Process design
Page 81: A number of the questions in this chapter were inspired by Dee Hock, founder of VISA, and originator of the theory of chaordic organizations.

Chapter 3: Question design
Page 108: Citation. Einstein is often quoted for having said this, though there is no evidence for this.
Page 110: Model: The path to dialogue comes from William Isaacs's book *Dialogue*. We have made a visualization of the model.
Page 112: Model: The decision-making diamond stems from Sam Kaner's *The Facilitator's Guide to Participatory Decision-Making*. We have simplified it and focus solely on the question's function and placement in time.
Page 116: Model: The architecture of good questions was inspired by the article *The Art of Powerful Questions* by Eric E. Vogt, Juanita Brown, and David Isaacs. They build on the work of Sally Ann Roth. We have created the

visual model for "Question structure" and changed the headings from "More powerful questions" and "Less powerful questions" to "Narrow questions" and "Broad questions." We have inverted the triangle so that the tip is at the bottom ("narrow questions") and the base of the triangle is at the top ("broad questions"). This model was further developed with permission from Juanita Brown.
Page 134: Question test. Inspiration for this also stems from "The Art of Powerful Questions." Taking the article's test questions as a starting point, we have compiled our list and added new questions.

Chapter 4: Template design
Page 173: The Business Model Canvas. Developed by Yves Pigneur and Alexander Osterwalder. Described in their book *Business Model Generation*. Used here in a simplified version with permission from Alexander Osterwalder. We show another two possible versions of the generator. Both are our "imagined" examples.
Page 174: SWOT matrix. There is no consensus as to who originally created this model. Many attribute it to Albert Humphrey, who in the 1960s and '70s worked at the Stanford Research Institute.

Page 174: The Gameplan was developed by David Sibbet and the Grove Consultants International. Used in a simplified version with permission from David Sibbet.
Page 175: Empathy map. Developed by Dave Gray. Used in a simplified version with permission from Dave Gray.
Page 175: Boston Matrix. Developed by Bruce Henderson from Boston Consulting Group in 1970. Used in a simplified version.

Chapter 6: System visualization
Page 208: Review of "social systems," "communication," and "autopoiesis" is based on Niklas Luhmann's *Social Systems* (1995).
Page 214: Review of "observation" is based on Niklas Luhmann's *Sociale systemer* (2000) and Niels Åkerstrøm Andersen's *Diskursive analysestrategier* (1999).
Page 218: Our definition of group learning builds on Carsten Ohm and Ole Qvist-Sørensen's thesis *Group Learning* (2000).
Page 220: The idea of the visual learning arena was inspired by the article "The Learning Group: From Theory to Practice," Ole Qvist-Sørensen, *Unge Pædagoger* (2003).

Great books

Process design, facilitation and visual facilitation

Graphic Facilitation. David Sibbet (2006). Grove. The first book on graphic facilitation.

Visual Teams. David Sibbet (2010). Wiley. The first book of four in the Visual Facilitation series by the pioneer of graphic facilitation.

The Facilitator's Guide to Participatory Decision-Making. Sam Kaner et al. (2007). Jossey-Bass. A primer in the art of facilitating large-scale processes towards joint decisions.

Facilitering. Ib Ravn (2011). Hans Reitzels Forlag. How facilitation can be used in any meeting or other assembly.

The brain, visualization, drawing, and illustration

Brain Rules. John Medina (2010). Pear Press. 12 rules about how the brain works, including how vision trumps other senses.

Visual Language: Global Communication for the 21st Century. Robert Horn (1998). Macro VU Press. One of the pioneers of the field, showing why and how visual language works.

UZMO: Thinking With Your Pen. Martin Haussmann (2017). Redline. Describes, among other things, how you can present thoughts and ideas with pen and paper.

The Sketchnote Handbook. Mike Rohde (2013). Peachpit Press. A book to help you take visual notes.

Back of the Napkin. Dan Roam (2008). Penguin. Shows how you can solve problems and sell ideas with simple sketches.

The Graphic Facilitator's Guide. Brandy Agerbeck (2012). Loosetooth.com Library. How to use listening, thinking, and drawing to make meaning.

Generative Scribing, Kelvy Bird (2018). Presencing Institute Press. Presents visualization as a social art form.

The Doodle Revolution. Sunni Brown (2014). Portfolio/Penguin. There is no such thing as a mindless doodle.

Steal Like an Artist. Austin Kleon (2012). Workman Publishing Company Inc. How to unlock your creativity.

Asking questions

The Art of Powerful Questions. Eric E. Vogt, Juanita Brown, and David Isaacs (2003). Whole Systems Associates. An article illustrating what makes questions good.

A More Beautiful Question. Warren Berger (2014). Bloomsbury. How questions and innovation are connected.

Metaphors

Metaphors We Live By. Georg Lakoff and Mark Johnson (1980/2003). University of Chicago Press. How metaphors are part of our thinking and being in the world.

Images of Organization. Gareth Morgan (1997). Sage. A primer in organization theory that describes the strengths and weaknesses of using image metaphors in organizations.

Storyboards

The Art of the Storyboard. John Hart (1999). Focal Press. Reviews the origin, development, use, and construction of storyboards.

Visual tools and presentation techniques

Business Model Generation. Alexander Osterwalder and Yves Pigneur (2010). Wiley. Describes how a visual tool can help you design a business model.

Value Proposition Design. Alexander Osterwalder et al. (2014). Wiley. How a visual tool can help you develop valuable products and services for your business.

Design a Better Business. Patrick van der Pijl (2016). Wiley. About Visual tools and methods of designing better companies.

Bikablo 2.0 (2012). Bikablo® akademie. A catalog of icons and templates for processes large and small.

Game Storming. Dave Gray, Sunni Brown, and James Macanufo (2010). O'Reilly. Exercises to develop valuable creative processes.

Slideology. Nancy Duarte (2008). O'Reilly. A book about presentations and the interplay between good narrative and the right visualization.

Social systems theory, systems thinking, and change management

Social Systems. Niklas Luhmann (1995). Stanford University Press. Luhmann's principle work, addressing how we can analyze all types of social contact.

Diskursive analysestrategier. Niels Åkerstrøm Andersen (1999). Nyt fra Samfundsvidenskaberne. Theories on observation of meaning formation.

Iagttagelse og blindhed: Om organisation, fornuft og utopi. Ole Thyssen (2000). Handelshøjskolens Forlag. About our observation of the world.

Leading from the Emerging Future. Otto Scharmer and Katrin Keufer (2013). Berrett-Koehler. A guide to creating a new sustainable economy.

The 5th Discipline. Peter Senge (1990/2003). Random House. A primer in creating a learning organization.

Dialogue: The Art of Thinking Together. William Isaacs (1999). Doubleday/Random House. About how to approach questions and listening.

Open Space Technology. Harrison Owen (2008). Berrett Koehler. A method for large scale meetings.

Communities of Practice. Etienne Wenger (1998). Cambridge University Press. About social learning systems.

Start with Why. Simon Sinek (2009). Portfolio. Why "why" matters most.

Change by Design. Tim Brown (2009). How design thinking transforms organizations and inspires innovation.

In the making

Enabling Clarity. Transform your work with the power of visual tools. Holger Nils Pohl. To be published end 2019. Presents the Clarity Framework (Understand, Create, Share) with an all new metrics for identifying various types of visual tools.

Business Model Shift: 6 New Ways to Add Value for Customers. Patrick van der Pijl. To be published spring 2020.

Acknowledgments

Thanks to Natalka and Mads for long talks, support, and gentle pushes in the right direction. Thank you, Aleksandra, Herman, Lukas, and Luigi for enriching our lives. Thanks to Lennart, Birgit, Ludmilla, Liselotte, Bue, Anne, Asbjørn, Gitte, and Ulrik for always participating in everything.

Thank you, Sofie, for your enormous work with the unbelievable number of illustrations of every size, for your always sharp and relevant input, your contagious engagement, and your ability to draw until we cry from laughing. Thanks to Thomas for his consistently expert sparring and to Ann-Sofie for reading and making linguistic improvements. Thanks to Thomas Ulrik for good partnership, the ability to ask us good questions, and for providing this book design. Thanks to Brigita, Ida, Hans Henrik, Anne, Brian, and Marius.

Thanks for the many decisive meetings, conversations: Bliss Browne, Lotte Darsø, Uffe Elbæk, Toke Møller, David Sibbet, Dee Hock, Juanita Brown and David Isaacs, Tom Cummings, Tim Merry, Tatiana Glad, Peter Senge, Otto Scharmer, and Patrick van der Pijl.

Thank you to everyone we have met, worked with, and learned from: Julian Burton, Reinhard Kuchenmüller, Marianne Stifel, Yuri Engelhardt, Lesley Salmon-Zhu, Robert Horn, Nancy Margulies, Dan Roam, Tom Wujec, Lee Lefever, Tim Haudan, Brandy Agerbeck,

Deirdre Crowley, Dave Gray, Nancy Duarte, Sunni Brown, Dennis Luijer, Guido Neuland, Martin Haussmann, and Holger Nils Pohl. And thanks to Mike Rohde, Austin Kleon, Alexander Osterwalder, and Yves Pigneur for bringing the visual message to a wider audience.

Over the years we have worked with a broad array of innovative organizations with inventive, tireless visionaries who dared to dive into something new despite the risk of failure; thanks to you: Ove Munch Ovesen (Novo Nordisk), Allan Vendelboe (Ballerup Municipality), Helena Nilsson (IKEA), Lisbeth Bech (Novozymes), Mads Kjaer (Kjaer Group), Marianne Jacobsen Werth (WWF), Stephan Singer (WWF), Johan Sigsgaard (A.P. Moller – Maersk), Susanne Nour (Institute for Human Rights), Ida Juhler (Gentofte Municipality), Annelise Goldstein (Novo Nordisk), Lars Fruergaard (Novo Nordisk), Lene Einang Flang (NRK), Danell Mc Dowel (IKEA), Stefan Krysen (IKEA), Virginie Aimard (UNU), Søren Lybecker (DTU), Grith Boesen (Novo Nordisk), Christine Antorini (Danish Ministry of Education), Lars Even Rasmussen (A.P. Moller – Maersk), Julija Voitiekute (A.P. Moller – Maersk), Christian Larsen (GEA), Majken Bønnelykke (LEGO), John Goodwin (LEGO), Christoph Eisenhardt (Roche), and Donato Carparelli (Schindler).

Many thanks to the organizations that contributed a case study for the book:

A.P. Moller – Maersk (Julija Voitiekute and Michael Ritter Christiansen), Danish Ministry of Education (Christine Antorini), Metro Service and Copenhagen Light Rail (Rebekka Nymark and Louise Høst), and IKEA (Stefan Krysen and Henrik Elm).

Great thanks to all of you who made time to give us valuable feedback along the way: Jens Rasmussen, Lotte Darsø, Ea Eskildsen, Elisabeth Mesterton Graae, Julija Voitiekute, Lene Einang Flang, Ove Munch Ovesen, Lars Kolind, Christer Lidzelius, Søren Lybecker, Anne Skare Nielsen, Monica Nissen, Matti Straub-Fischer, Jacob Storch, Carsten Ohm, Henrik Challis, and Rune Baastrup.

Thank you to Nordic International for the thorough job of translating the book from Danish to English, to Bliss Brown for reviewing and shortening the book, to Robert Bell for final copyediting before handing it over to Wiley. *Tusind tak*! To Patrick van der Pijl for recommending the book to Wiley and to Richard Narramore from Wiley for believing in this book. To our team at Wiley: thank you Victoria Anllo, Vicki Adang, Samantha Hartley, and Amy Handy for the great work in the final stretch toward a print-ready book.

And last, but not least, THANK YOU, dear reader, for picking up this book.

Index